TEACHING STUDENTS
WITH
COMMUNICATION
DISORDERS

A PRACTICAL APPROACH TO SPECIAL EDUCATION FOR EVERY TEACHER

The Fundamentals of Special Education
A Practical Guide for Every Teacher

The Legal Foundations of Special Education
A Practical Guide for Every Teacher

Effective Assessment for Students With Special Needs
A Practical Guide for Every Teacher

Effective Instruction for Students With Special Needs
A Practical Guide for Every Teacher

*Working With Families and Community Agencies to Support
    Students With Special Needs*
A Practical Guide for Every Teacher

Public Policy, School Reform, and Special Education
A Practical Guide for Every Teacher

Teaching Students With Sensory Disabilities
A Practical Guide for Every Teacher

Teaching Students With Medical, Physical, and Multiple Disabilities
A Practical Guide for Every Teacher

Teaching Students With Learning Disabilities
A Practical Guide for Every Teacher

Teaching Students With Communication Disorders
A Practical Guide for Every Teacher

Teaching Students With Emotional Disturbance
A Practical Guide for Every Teacher

Teaching Students With Mental Retardation
A Practical Guide for Every Teacher

Teaching Students With Gifts and Talents
A Practical Guide for Every Teacher

TEACHING STUDENTS WITH COMMUNICATION DISORDERS

A Practical Guide for Every Teacher

JIM YSSELDYKE
BOB ALGOZZINE

CORWIN PRESS
A SAGE Publications Company
Thousand Oaks, California

For information:

Corwin Press
A Sage Publications Company
2455 Teller Road
Thousand Oaks, California 91320
www.corwinpress.com

Sage Publications Ltd.
1 Oliver's Yard
55 City Road
London EC1Y 1SP
United Kingdom

Sage Publications India Pvt. Ltd.
B-42, Panchsheel Enclave
Post Box 4109
New Delhi 110 017 India

Printed in the United States of America

Library of Congress Cataloging-in-Publication Data

Ysseldyke, James E.
Teaching students with communication disorders: A practical guide for every teacher / James E. Ysseldyke & Bob Algozzine.
p. cm.
Includes bibliographical references and index.
ISBN 1-4129-3950-X (cloth)
ISBN 1-4129-3903-8 (pbk.)
    1. Children with disabilities--Education—United States. 2. Language arts—Remedial teaching—United States. 3. Speech disorders in children--United States. 4. Communicative disorders in children—United States. 5. Special education—United States. 6. Special education teachers—Training of—United States. I. Algozzine, Robert. II. Title.
LC4028.Y78 2006
371.91'4--dc22

                                                            2005037826

This book is printed on acid-free paper.

06   07   08   09   10   9   8   7   6   5   4   3   2   1

Acquisitions Editor:	Kylee M. Liegl
Editorial Assistant:	Nadia Kashper
Production Editor:	Denise Santoyo
Copy Editor:	Marilyn Power Scott
Typesetter:	C&M Digitals (P) Ltd.
Indexer:	Kathy Paparchontis
Cover Designer:	Michael Dubowe

Contents

About *A Practical Approach to Special*
Education for Every Teacher   vii
    Acknowledgments   viii

About the Authors   xi

Self-Assessment 1   1

Introduction to *Teaching Students With*
Communication Disorders   7

1. What Are Communication Disorders?   9
    Speech Disorders   9
    Language Disorders   10
       Language Form, Function, and Content   10
    Criteria for Identification   11

2. What Characteristics Are Associated With
    Communication Disorders?   13
    Cognitive   13
    Academic   14
    Physical   14
    Behavioral   15
    Communication   15

3. How Do Teachers Teach Students With
    Communication Disorders?   17
    Reducing Speech Problems   18
    Reducing Language Problems   20
    Reducing Interpersonal Problems   27

4. What Trends and Issues Influence How We Teach
   Students With Communication Disorders?   31

5. Communication Disorders in Perspective   35
   Team Approach to Providing Services   35
   Pulling Students Out of the Classroom   36
   Combating Negative Stereotypes   37
   Tips to Improve Communication   38

6. What Have We Learned?   39
   Key Points   42
   Key Vocabulary   43

Self-Assessment 2   47

Answer Key for Self-Assessments   53

On Your Own   55

Resources   57
   Books   57
   Journals and Articles   57
   Organizations   58

References   61

Index   63

About
A Practical Approach to Special Education for Every Teacher

S pecial education means specially designed instruction for students with unique learning needs. Students receive special education for many reasons. Students with disabilities such as mental retardation, hearing impairments (including deafness), speech or language impairments, visual impairments (including blindness), emotional disturbance, orthopedic impairments, autism, traumatic brain injury, other health impairments, or specific learning disabilities are entitled to special education services. Students who are gifted and talented also receive special education. Special education services are delivered in many settings, including regular classes, resource rooms, and separate classes. The 13 books of this collection will help you teach students with disabilities and those with gifts and talents. Each book focuses on a specific area of special education and can be used individually or in conjunction with all or some of the other books. Six of the books provide the background and content knowledge you need in order to work effectively with all students with unique learning needs:

Book 1: The Fundamentals of Special Education

Book 2: The Legal Foundations of Special Education

Book 3: Effective Assessment for Students With Special Needs

Book 4: Effective Instruction for Students With Special Needs

Book 5: Working With Families and Community Agencies to Support Students With Special Needs

Book 6: Public Policy, School Reform, and Special Education

Seven of the books focus on teaching specific groups of students who receive special education:

Book 7:   Teaching Students With Sensory Disabilities

Book 8:   Teaching Students With Medical, Physical, and Multiple Disabilities

Book 9:   Teaching Students With Learning Disabilities

Book 10: Teaching Students With Communication Disorders

Book 11: Teaching Students With Emotional Disturbance

Book 12: Teaching Students With Mental Retardation

Book 13: Teaching Students With Gifts and Talents

All of the books in *A Practical Approach to Special Education for Every Teacher* will help you to make a difference in the lives of all students, especially those with unique learning needs.

ACKNOWLEDGMENTS

The approach we take in *A Practical Approach to Special Education for Every Teacher* is an effort to change how professionals learn about special education. The 13 separate books are a result of prodding from our students and from professionals in the field to provide a set of materials that "cut to the chase" in teaching them about students with disabilities and about building the capacity of systems to meet those students' needs. Teachers told us that in their classes they always confront students with special learning needs and students their school district has assigned a label to (e.g., students with learning disabilities). Our students and the professionals we worked with wanted a very practical set of texts that gave them the necessary **information about the students** (e.g., federal definitions, student characteristics) and specific **information on** *what to do about* **the students** (assessment and teaching strategies, approaches that work). They also wanted the opportunity to purchase parts of textbooks, rather than entire texts, to learn what they needed.

The production of this collection would not have been possible without the support and assistance of many colleagues. Professionals associated with Corwin Press—Faye Zucker, Kylee Liegl, Robb Clouse—helped us work through the idea of introducing special education differently, and their support in helping us do it is deeply appreciated.

Faye Ysseldyke and Kate Algozzine, our children, and our grandchildren also deserve recognition. They have made the problems associated with the project very easy to diminish, deal with, or dismiss. Every day in every way, they enrich our lives and make us better. We are grateful for them.

About the Authors

Jim Ysseldyke, PhD, is Birkmaier Professor in the Department of Educational Psychology, director of the School Psychology Program, and director of the Center for Reading Research at the University of Minnesota. Widely requested as a staff developer and conference speaker, he brings more than 30 years of research and teaching experience to educational professionals around the globe.

As the former director of the federally funded National Center on Educational Outcomes, Ysseldyke conducted research and provided technical support that helped to boost the academic performance of students with disabilities and improve school assessment techniques nationally. Today he continues to work to improve the education of students with disabilities.

The author of more than 300 publications on special education and school psychology, Ysseldyke is best known for his textbooks on assessment, effective instruction, issues in special education, and other cutting-edge areas of education and school psychology. With *A Practical Approach to Special Education for Every Teacher,* he seeks to equip educators with practical knowledge and methods that will help them to better engage students in exploring—and meeting—all their potentials.

Bob Algozzine, PhD, is Professor in the Department of Educational Leadership at the University of North Carolina at Charlotte and project codirector of the U.S. Department of Education–supported Behavior and Reading Improvement Center. With 25 years of research experience and extensive first-hand knowledge of teaching students classified as seriously emotionally disturbed (and other equally useless terms), Algozzine is a uniquely qualified staff developer, conference speaker, and teacher of behavior management and effective teaching courses.

As an active partner and collaborator with professionals in the Charlotte-Mecklenburg schools in North Carolina and as an editor of several journals focused on special education, Algozzine keeps his finger on the pulse of current special education practice. He has written more than 250 manuscripts on special education topics, authoring many popular books and textbooks on how to manage emotional and social behavior problems. Through *A Practical Approach to Special Education for Every Teacher*, Algozzine hopes to continue to help improve the lives of students with special needs—and the professionals who teach them.

Self-Assessment 1

Before you begin this book, check your knowledge of the content being covered. Choose the best answer for each of the following questions.

1. The two main types of communication disorders are

   a. Speech disorders and articulation problems

   b. Speech disorders and language disorders

   c. Receptive language disorders and expressive language disorders

   d. Written expression disorders and expressive language disorders

2. The absence or abnormal production of vocal quality, pitch, loudness, resonance, or duration is known as a (or an)

   a. Articulation disorder

   b. Fluency disorder

   c. Morphology disorder

   d. Voice disorder

3. Which of the following is NOT related to language disorders?

   a. Articulation

   b. Function

   c. Form

   d. Content

4. When a student is unable to identify appropriate pictures when word names are provided, that student might have difficulty with

   a. Morphology

   b. Pragmatics

   c. Semantics

   d. Syntax

5. The caseload of a speech-language pathologist consists primarily of students who receive services for _____ or _____ disorders.

   a. Morphology, phonology

   b. Receptive, expressive

   c. Articulation, fluency

   d. Articulation, language

6. The most common fluency disorder is

   a. Slow speech

   b. Stuttering

   c. Inappropriate repetition

   d. Self-interruption

7. The most common accepted term for a communication disorders professional is

   a. Speech-language pathologist

   b. Teachers of the speech and language impaired

   c. Speech therapist

   d. Speech correction teacher

8. Which of the following is NOT an appropriate suggestion for teachers working with students with communication disorders?

   a. Use areas of strength to compensate for weakness.

   b. Provide good speech models.

   c. Tell students to "take their time" when they stutter.

   d. Value speech and language diversity.

9. To improve the use of grammar, teachers should focus on

   a. Sentence structure

   b. Expressive language

   c. Pronunciation

   d. Meaning

10. A teacher completes a series of checklists concerning Sara's speech patterns, and the speech-language pathologist talks informally with Sara. These steps are part of the _____ process.

    a. Special education

    b. Referral

    c. Evaluation

    d. Information

11. The Peabody is a test of

    a. Language comprehension

    b. Articulation

    c. Phonology

    d. Vocabulary

12. Which of the following is a tactic for helping students to overcome social and emotional problems?

   a. Convey information with praise.

   b. Be careful to praise, not embarrass, students.

   c. Praise the obvious.

   d. All of the above.

13. Which of the following should be taken into account when deciding whether a student needs special education for communication difficulties?

   a. Intelligence

   b. Cultural differences

   c. Behavior problems

   d. Grades

14. The organization for communication disorders professionals is the

   a. American Academy of Speech Correction

   b. National Association of Communication Disorders

   c. Speech and Language Association of America

   d. American Speech-Language-Hearing Association

15. Students who are pulled out of their classrooms for speech or language services should be pulled out during

   a. Independent practice time

   b. Favorite subjects

   c. Core courses

   d. None of the above

16. Which of the following is an appropriate word for describing a student with communication disorders?

    a. Language disordered

    b. Language delayed

    c. Language deviant

    d. None of the above

REFLECTION

After you answer the multiple-choice questions, provide a short answer to the following questions:

- In what areas are students with communication disorders likely to experience difficulties?
- What is the difference between language and speech disorders, and which is more common?
- What is your opinion regarding the delivery of speech and language services—should they be conducted in the classroom or in a special education setting?

Introduction to Teaching Students With Communication Disorders

Peggy speaks clearly when her teacher calls on her for information, but some of the words don't sound exactly right when she answers. "Keep away fwom me, you wascally wabbit" is one of her favorite sayings. Although this type of substitution is common for children in kindergarten and first grade, it is beginning to cause problems for Peggy because her classmates are making fun of the way she says things, and her parents and teachers are concerned that it is no longer appropriate for her age.

⟨୨⟩

Sally's teacher describes her speech as "just like a much younger child." She mispronounces words, omits sounds, and sometimes speaks too quickly to be easily understood. A speech-language pathologist described Sally's problem as a speech fluency disorder and recommended that she work on producing proper sounds more than on other areas of speech or language. She encouraged Sally's parents to help by using sentences with word pairs that illustrate the importance of pronunciation and speech sounds (e.g., "Did they present the present?" or "The graduate will graduate this spring") and by being models of proper articulation when they speak to her rather than calling attention to her dysfluencies.

(Continued)

(Continued)

> **Irving** is a high school student with a stuttering problem. Although his written work is outstanding, Irving is reluctant to volunteer answers in class, participate in group discussions, or give oral presentations. His stuttering is much worse when he is talking to people he doesn't know.
>
> ⌒⌒
>
> Grammatical errors (such as "she run to store") and immature language usage (such as "go now") are the most representative characteristics of **John's** language. He seldom uses complete sentences and often mixes, incorrectly uses, or omits parts of speech in his written and expressive language. He has a poor speaking vocabulary, and his language problems are beginning to cause serious problems with his peers.

Many students receiving special education have communication disorders. Some have such severe impairments that they need assistive devices, such as computerized speech aids, to communicate with others. Most, however, like Peggy, Sally, Irving, and John, have milder impairments. The special education category of Communication Disorders includes students whose problems producing speech or using language symbols interfere significantly with their ability to communicate. In most school districts, speech-language pathologists work collaboratively with classroom teachers to provide services to students with communication disorders.

1

What Are Communication Disorders?

There are two types of **communication disorders**: Those that affect speech (speech disorders) and those that affect language (language disorders). Problems producing speech sounds (articulation), controlling sounds that are produced (voice), and controlling the rate and rhythm of speech (fluency) are generally considered **speech disorders**. Problems with using proper forms of language (phonology, morphology, syntax), using the content of language (semantics), and using the functions of language (pragmatics) are generally considered **language disorders**.

SPEECH DISORDERS

The American Speech-Language-Hearing Association (ASHA; 1982) has developed formal definitions of each speech disorder:

Articulation disorder is defined as "the abnormal production of speech sounds" (p. 949). When a student says, "The wabbit wan don the woad," or "poon" for "spoon," or "gog" for "dog," he or she may be using spoken language appropriately but is not producing sounds correctly.

Voice disorder is defined as "the absence or abnormal production of vocal quality, pitch, loudness, resonance, and/or duration" (p. 949). Students with voice disorders sometimes sound hoarse or speak loudly or in a high or low pitch.

Fluency disorder is defined as "the abnormal flow of verbal expression, characterized by impaired rate and rhythm which may be accompanied by struggle behavior" (p. 949). S-saying th-the f-first s-sound o-of a-a w-word and th-then s-saying th-the w-word illustrates this problem.

LANGUAGE DISORDERS

All other communication problems are considered language disorders. ASHA (1982) defines three kinds of language disorders—specifically, problems related to form, content, and function. Language **form** refers to the utterance or sentence structure of what is said—phonology, morphology, and syntax. Language **content** refers to meanings of words and sentences, including abstract concepts—semantics. Language **function** refers to the context in which language can be used and the purpose of communication—pragmatics. Problems can be **receptive** (related to hearing, listening to, or receiving language) and **expressive** (related to producing or expressing language).

Language Form, Function, and Content

Phonology is concerned with the smallest units of language (phonemes or speech sounds); **morphology** is concerned with the smallest units of meaningful language (morphemes or words and parts of words); and **syntax** is concerned with combining language units into meaningful phrases, clauses, or sentences (grammatically correct language). Problems with phonology, morphology, and syntax are evident when students are unable to differentiate sounds (/b/ versus /p/), words (cat or cap), or grammatically correct sentences ("John go to the movies" versus "John goes to the movies") or to produce appropriate sounds, words, or sentences.

Semantics is concerned with word and message meanings (vocabulary, comprehension, following directions). Problems with semantics are evident when students are unable to identify appropriate pictures when word names are provided ("Find the grapes"), answer simple questions ("Are apples fruits?"), follow directions ("Draw a line over the third box"), tell how words or messages are similar or different ("How are apples, oranges, and pears alike?"), or understand abstract concepts ("What is love?").

Pragmatics is concerned with the use and function of language in varying settings (i.e., following social conversational rules). Problems with pragmatics are evident when students are unable to use language in social situations to express feelings, create or understand images, give or request information, or direct actions of listeners.

CRITERIA FOR IDENTIFICATION

Professionals use a number of criteria to identify communication disorders, and they may be concerned with receptive as well as expressive problems. Identification of speech problems is usually accomplished by listening to oral reading or speech samples or by asking students questions. Most language disorders are identified by poor performance on language tests or from analyses of written and oral schoolwork.

2

What Characteristics Are Associated With Communication Disorders?

F ederal guidelines do not separate speech problems from language problems. This causes state departments to not differentiate students with speech problems from those with language problems in their counts of students requiring special education. Yet students with speech problems demonstrate communication characteristics different from those demonstrated by students with language problems. Speech problems are evidenced in the production of speech (e.g., misarticulations, abnormal flow of expression). Language problems are evidenced in the form, content, and use of receptive and expressive language (e.g., vocabulary, grammar). The caseload of a speech-language pathologist consists primarily of students who receive services for articulation or language disorders. Students with voice and fluency disorders compose less than 5 percent of a typical caseload.

COGNITIVE

There are two schools of thought about the extent to which students who have speech and language problems show cognitive difficulties. According to one of them, some students do have cognitive difficulties, as shown by poor performance on intelligence tests, particularly on verbal intelligence tests. Their development of cognitive skills (identifying similarities among objects or concepts, understanding sentences and words)—which is heavily dependent on language—is hampered by their language problems. The competing view holds that students with communication disorders have normal or average intellectual functioning but appear deficient because their speech and language problems affect their performance on intelligence tests.

It may be that difficulties communicating cause cognitive difficulties, or it may be that cognitive difficulties cause communication difficulties. The research is not clear. The causation may run in either direction, depending on the individual student. The close relationship between communication and cognitive development can make it difficult to determine a student's actual needs.

ACADEMIC

School is a verbal-symbolic environment. Throughout the school years, especially in kindergarten and first grade, academic performance is highly dependent on students' skill in listening, following directions, and comprehending. Students are expected to understand and act in response to verbal symbols and spoken language. Students who have speech and language problems usually experience difficulties in reading, social studies, language arts, and other subjects that depend heavily on understanding verbal and written communication skills.

PHYSICAL

Students with certain conditions—cerebral palsy, cleft palate or other kinds of oral-facial disorders, and some types of mental retardation—may experience speech and language difficulties as well as physical problems. But for most students with speech and language impairments, there is no specific correspondence between physical appearance or functioning and speech or language functioning.

BEHAVIORAL

Communication serves a social function. Students with speech and language difficulties, by the nature of their difficulties, often call attention to themselves. If a student's speech or language is obviously different from that of peers, then teachers, adults, and peers often behave differently toward the student. They may pay more attention to the way in which the student says something than to what the student says. Peers may ridicule a student whose speech is noticeably different, and this can cause emotional problems. Students who have speech and language difficulties may withdraw from social situations, be rejected in social situations, and ultimately, may suffer from a loss of self confidence.

COMMUNICATION

The communication characteristics of students with speech and language disorders are a function of the specific kind of disorder. For example, students with speech problems related to articulation mispronounce words or parts of words; they may have difficulty being understood. But the nature of speech-language problems varies greatly. Diane's articulation problem may be one of omitting sounds; Sam's, one of distorting sounds.

Voice Problems

Voice disorders can appear in quality, loudness, or pitch. At times the disorder is of such magnitude that the student's speech irritates teachers and other students. You can imagine what it's like to have a student with a squeaky or a loud voice in a classroom.

Fluency Problems

Students with fluency disorders demonstrate interruptions in the timing or rhythm of their speech, which can frustrate both speaker and listener. The most common fluency disorder is stuttering. When adults are asked whether they have ever stuttered, about 5 percent say they have; about 4 percent of these self-correct, so the incidence of stuttering is about 1 percent (Mizuko, 2002). At one time, stuttering was attributed to psychological problems. Although this explanation has not been entirely cast aside, researchers suspect that a combination of biological, psychological, and environmental factors predispose a person to stutter. New evidence suggests that stuttering may be caused by a physiological breakdown of brain mechanisms or possibly by excessive tension in the vocal cords.

Language Problems

Students with language disorders may demonstrate difficulty combining sounds to form words or combining words to form structurally correct sentences. They generally have difficulty using language to express themselves or to understand others.

3

How Do Teachers Teach Students With Communication Disorders?

S tudents with communication disorders often receive special education from people trained to address speech and language problems. The name assigned to these professionals varies. The most common and accepted term over the years has been **speech-language pathologist**. This name causes concern within the profession because it implies a medical orientation that often is inappropriate for people working in schools. "Teachers of the speech and language impaired" is a term being used in some areas. This term also causes problems. First, teachers don't like the word "the" in the title because it refers to students as the disorder and not as students. It also places communication disorders in a class by themselves because no other specialized service has such a specific title.

In this book, *speech-language pathologist* is the term being used for people who work with individuals with speech and language impairments. They may be called something else where you live and work. We are not that concerned about what these professionals are called; our interest is in what they do to provide assistance to students and other teachers of students with communication disorders.

Speech-language pathologists hold master's degrees in communication disorders, and most have certifications of clinical competence from ASHA. They are certified by state departments of education, much like special education and elementary, middle, and high school teachers. Speech-language pathologists conduct assessments and provide therapy based on their results. When they work in schools, they sometimes function as itinerant specialists, spending one or two days a week in each building to which they are assigned.

In larger districts, speech-language pathologists may be assigned to just one or two schools. Increasingly, these professionals are working collaboratively with classroom teachers, helping them plan instruction for students with speech and language problems. This is particularly true in school districts emphasizing inclusionary programs in which students with disabilities are taught in the same classrooms as their neighbors and peers. A list of tips for classroom teachers working with students with communication disorders is provided in *Table 3.1*. The speech-language pathologist can offer advice and assistance in developing these general interventions. More specific suggestions for classroom activities are presented in the following sections.

REDUCING SPEECH PROBLEMS

Speech-language pathologists work closely with teachers to provide services to students who have speech disorders, especially those related to articulation of speech sounds and, to a lesser extent, fluency of speech or unusual voice quality. The goal for most of these teachers is to provide good speech models, accepting environments, and opportunities for students to practice newly developed speech skills (Lewis & Doorlag, 1991). The following tactics will help you improve these areas of speech production:

1. Provide good models of appropriate speech. Speak clearly with appropriate pronunciation and encourage students to demonstrate appropriate speech without calling attention to a classmate's errors. For example, when Peggy jokingly told her teacher, "Keep away fwom me, you wascally wabbit," the teacher

Table 3.1   Top Ten Tips for Teachers of Students With Communication Disorders

1. Integrate appropriate language development activities into all curriculum areas.

2. Create a supportive environment where communication is fostered and valued.

3. Provide opportunities during the instructional day for students to practice skills being learned in therapy.

4. Use areas of strength to compensate for weaknesses.

5. Value speech and language diversity.

6. Arrange activities in which students use language for various purposes (e.g., oral book reports, mock job interviews, speeches, surveys) with various audiences (e.g., another class at the same grade level, class at another grade level, family members).

7. Provide good speech models.

8. Provide opportunities during academic instruction for free exchange of ideas and discussions about what is being taught.

9. Organize classroom space with at least one area reserved for students to talk to each other.

10. Consider developmental levels before making referrals for outside assistance.

responded by saying, "Oh no you don't, I'll get you, you rascally rabbit," rather than pointing out the mistake.

2. Focus on quantity more than quality of speech. Many speech production problems tend to become worse when teachers and students call attention to them. Attending to the content of communication more than the carrier often helps speech problems from becoming more serious.

3. Provide opportunities for practice. Many students with speech and language problems receive special education from speech-language pathologists in settings other than their general education classrooms. Teachers who encourage these students to practice what they are learning in the special education settings find that problems improve more quickly. For example, when Sally was working with the speech-language pathologist on differentiating words by paying attention to syllable accents, her classroom teacher organized a classroom word game in which students picked the right word from orally presented clues (e.g., "You bring me to a party? Am I present [prĕz ˊ ˊnt] or present [prĭ zentˊ]?").

REDUCING LANGUAGE PROBLEMS

Language disorders are most likely to be the concern of speech-language pathologists working collaboratively with classroom teachers. Problems in receptive and expressive language involving proper use of vocabulary and grammatical structure are common in most classrooms. Many students with learning disabilities exhibit language problems. The following tactics will help you improve the use of language in students with communication problems.

1. **To improve use of grammar, focus on meaning.** Sentence meanings are influenced by the use of punctuation and intonation. Playing word and sentence games can help students with language problems see the value of grammar and inflection. Have students say the following words in at least two different ways that convey positive and negative meanings: *turkey, school, love, monsters.* Have students identify the multiple meanings evident in the following sentences and then have them construct some of their own:

   Let's talk turkey.

   The man decided on the train.

   They fed her dog biscuits.

2. **To improve vocabulary, focus on meaning.** Encourage students with language problems to ask about the meanings of words they don't understand.

3. **To improve vocabulary, combine gestures with verbal language.** Students with language problems may have difficulty understanding the meanings of prepositions, adverbs, and verbs. By acting out the meaning of *through, over, quickly,* and *struggled,* John's teacher helped him to understand a story she was reading to the class. She also had all her students act out words like *wiggle, shake, bounce, tumble,* and *spin* as they were learning them.

4. **To improve written expression, focus on quantity as well as quality in written work.** Encourage students to write as much as possible without concern for errors and to use their writings as a source for qualitative changes in their instruction. For example, place a picture (e.g., an art print, magazine page, or book illustration) on each students' desks and have them write about the pictures. After two or three minutes, have the students pass what has been written and their pictures to a classmate. Have them read what was written by the previous writer and add to what was written during the next writing segment (two to three minutes). Continue until at least four students have written about the pictures. Have them read by the final writer. Use the content in these stories as a basis for planning future instructional activities, such as using details, expressing emotions, and summarizing text.

5. **To improve written products, teach specific skills and have students monitor their written work.** Grammar is teachable, and written products are improved by using it appropriately. Correct grammatical usage (e.g., use of verbs, adverbs, adjectives, and proper tense) should be taught using teacher-guided practice lessons. Ask students to evaluate what they write ("Did I use verb tense appropriately?" "Can I use more adjectives or adverbs?" "Did I tell how the action was done?") and keep journals illustrating improvements in their written products.

6. **To improve vocabulary and word usage, use familiar words as building blocks.** Teach students to use familiar words to make new ones. For example, simply adding prefixes (*foot, afoot,* or *unable, unbeaten, uncertain, undo*) and suffixes (*quiet, quietly, quietness*) produces new parts of speech

and new words to expand vocabularies. Give spelling tests on the new words to improve the confidence of students with language problems in using their new words.

7. **To improve vocabulary and word usage, use acting games to teach meaning.** Choose an action (such as "Stand in one place," "Move from place to place," or "Make your face . . . ") and have students act out the meaning of appropriate words from their speaking and listening vocabularies. Here are some examples:

- *In One Place:* bend, bob, bounce, collapse, contract, droop, expand, flop, hang, lean, rock, shake, stretch, wiggle, wobble
- *From Place to Place:* amble, bop, crawl, dodge, evacuate, flail, gallop, hustle, limp, meander, prance, stamp, stumble, trot, wander
- *Make Your Face . . . blink, chew, cringe, frown, glare, grimace, grin, groan*
- *Make Your Legs and Feet . . . drag, kick, shuffle, scuff, stamp, stumble, tap*
- *Pantomime:* calling, crowing, crying, falling, hiccupping, howling, humming, giggling, sneezing, snickering, whistling
- *Dramatize:* boredom, conceit, contempt, disgust, envy, gratitude, happiness, horror, loneliness, shame, wonder

8. **To improve vocabulary and word usage, play word games.** Use a few of the following riddles as starters; have students make up some of their own as practice in building expressive vocabularies and using language.

- What is boring singing?   *Long song*
- What is a house mortgage?   *Home loan*
- What is a skinny hotel?   *Thin inn*
- What is a cheap medieval soldier?   *Tight knight*
- What is a chicken enclosure?   *Hen pen*

Give students a word (*four*) and have them change one letter at a time to make another word (*five*) after a specific number of steps. Make the task more difficult by eliminating some clues.

"Four"

Clue	Word
bad smell	_____ (foul)
chickens	_____ (fowl)
aluminum _____	_____ (foil)
do not pass	_____ (fail)
all _____ down	_____ (fall)
ate too much	_____ (full)
_____ 'er up	_____ (fill)
storage space	_____ (file)
It's hot	_____ (fire)

"Five"

Give students a word (*fa*) and have them create new words by adding letters. For example:

Start with *fa* and change it to other words by adding letters to the initial consonant.

Clue

    cost, charge

    before five

    picture _____

    well-known

    type of book

    after thirty-ninth

    normal actions

Word

    fa

    _____ (fee)

    _____ (four)

_____ (frame)

_____ (famous)

_____ (fiction)

_____ (fortieth)

_____ (functions)

Bringing Learning to Life: Identifying John's Communication Disorder

John's teacher was concerned about his communication problems and referred him to the school diagnostic team. In collaboration with a speech-language pathologist and a special education teacher, the team planned an evaluation of John's speech and language functioning. They used this information to decide if his problems were serious enough to warrant special education.

Speech Evaluation

John's classroom teacher completed a series of checklists used by the speech-language pathologist to provide information about the seriousness of speech problems. Here's an example of some of the items on it:

Student _____

Age _____

Grade _____

Teacher _____

Date of Evaluation _____

1. General Questions

   a. Can you understand what this student is saying? If not, give examples illustrating problems.

b. Does this student sound like other students in your room? If not, give examples illustrating differences.

c. Is what this student says appropriate to the situation in which it is said? If not, give examples illustrating problems.

d. Does this student struggle when communicating? If so, give examples illustrating problems.

e. Are there other indications of speech or language problems? If so, give illustrative examples.

f. Does this student's communication interfere with his or her participation in the classroom or socialization within the school environment?

2. Articulation (producing sounds)

Which of the following sounds does this student usually produce correctly?

___ /w/ as in *waiter*

___ /f/ as in *father*

___ /h/ as in *house*

___ /r/ as in *rat*

___ /ch/ as in *church*

___ /th/ as in *think*

___ /t/ as in *table*

___ /m/ as in *mother*

___ /b/ as in *balloon*

___ /1/ as in *lady*

___ /sh/ as in *show*

___ /th/ as in *those*

(Continued)

(Continued)

3. Voice Quality (controlling sounds)

What does this student's voice usually sound like?

__ pleasant

__ quiet

__ hoarse, raspy

__ nasal

__ not pleasant

__ not quiet

__ not hoarse, raspy

__ not nasal

4. Fluency (controlling rate and rhythm of speech)

What does this student's speech usually sound like?

__ few hesitations, repetitions, or added sounds

__ some hesitations, repetitions, or added sounds

__ many hesitations, repetitions, or added sounds

Language Evaluation

The speech-language pathologist administered some formal and informal tests to provide information about the seriousness of John's language problems. The following are some of the tests with which John's use of language form, content, and functions were evaluated.

1. Form (phonology, morphology, syntax)

Goldman-Fristoe Test of Articulation (Goldman & Fristoe, 2000)

Test for Auditory Comprehension of Language (Carrow-Woolfolk, 1999)

2. Content (semantics)

Assessment of Children's Language Comprehension (Foster, Giddan, & Stark, 1983)

Peabody Picture Vocabulary Test-Revised (Dunn & Dunn, 2000)

3. Function (pragmatics)

Observation of conversations with adults and peers

Role-playing conversations in different situations

Pragmatics checklist:

How often does this student engage the following language functions appropriately?

Function	Frequency		
	Very Seldom	*Sometimes*	*Very Often*
Greets others	1	2	3
Responds to requests	1	2	3
Relays messages	1	2	3
Asks for favors	1	2	3
Expresses feelings	1	2	3
Expresses disagreement	1	2	3
Compliments others	1	2	3
Expresses affection	1	2	3

REDUCING INTERPERSONAL PROBLEMS

Students with speech and language problems often experience difficulties with interpersonal interactions as a result of their communication problems. The following tactics will help students to overcome social and emotional problems:

1. **Praise accomplishments.** This approach is especially useful with students experiencing communication problems. Praise for genuine accomplishments is more effective than general, unspecified praise. Students with communication disorders are quick to recognize undeserved praise; they will view it as shallow and dishonest when it is delivered inappropriately. In judging when to praise, keep the student's past history and previous performances in mind; praise may seem appropriate and genuine to one student but greatly undeserved to another. The most effective praise is delivered when the student recognizes that it is in response to a genuine accomplishment.

2. **Convey information with praise.** Praise that provides specifics about a skill or accomplishment is more effective than praise that simply reflects status. For example, "Bill, that oral report was very clearly delivered" or "Thank you for slowing down when I gave you the signal we talked about" is more informative than "Bill, you received the highest grade in the class." Orient praise so that students can focus on their developing skills rather than on someone's approval of them.

3. **Focus praise on ability and effort.** Praise that identifies a student's ability and effort as the source of success is most effective. The statement should indicate that success was achieved because skills were used to complete a task with the right amount of effort.

4. **Be careful to praise, not embarrass, students.** Not all of your students have the same reactions to praise, especially those who may be sensitive to public attention. Many students with communication problems find even simple recognition of their skills and abilities embarrassing; elaborate reactions to their behavior can be personally discomforting. Be sure that when you praise a student, it will be perceived as rewarding by the recipient. Bear in mind that private praise is more effective than public praise that is embarrassing.

5. **Vary praise by developmental level.** Students learning new speech and language skills need more frequent praise than those practicing skills that have been acquired. Praise after a

selected number of responses or a specified time period is appropriate for new learning. Intermittent praise—less frequent random presentations—is more appropriate for later stages of learning.

6. Generate praise for the entire group. Students with communication problems often have low self-concepts and are reluctant to believe praise is true. To compensate, dispense praise to the whole group (or a select group) of students and in that context direct a specific good word to targeted students. Spend a minute or two quickly going around the classroom mentioning something positive about each student. Providing peers with comments like "nice handwriting," "beautiful shirt," "thanks for always being on time," and "great math today" may soften the extent to which students with communication disorders think they are singled out for specific praise for something they have done.

7. Praise the obvious. Take a little time on certain days, just before the students leave for home, to point out some of the day's positive occurrences. This tactic can become a joyful good-bye for each student and provide a final opportunity to strengthen developing skills at the end of the school day.

8. Use activities as substitutes for praise. A number of brief activities can be used to point out the positive qualities of a student. Careful selection of activities enables all students to benefit. The following examples illustrate verbal praise substitutes.

Teacher of the Day—Each day, select one student to be teacher. Have the student make all important decisions (such as time for recess and bathroom privileges) after consultation with the aide (the classroom teacher).

Student of the Week—Each week, randomly select a student to be the focus of peer praise. Classmates write down positive skills or characteristics of the target student, then incorporate them into a letter to take home at the end of the week.

VIP Bulletin Board—Take a photo of a student and place it on a bulletin board with a list of positive statements. Leave space for students to add other positive comments.

9. Communicate with families to extend praise. Involve families in instructional efforts. Have students with communication disorders use notebooks as diaries or scrapbooks of accomplishments. Buy several sizes and types of inexpensive notebooks so students can make more individualized choices. Send the notebooks home and have family members sign them as evidence of recognition of the students' achievements. Have parents periodically select favorite passages and review the strengths of each with their children.

4

What Trends and Issues Influence How We Teach Students With Communication Disorders?

S peech and language problems are common. In recent years, many more students have demonstrated speech and language characteristics that then have been served by special education. Deciding when a student with speech or language problems is in need of special education and who should be responsible for providing it are difficult issues that teachers and other professionals face each school year. They also must decide whether language differences common in students from other cultures are an appropriate basis for special education.

Many teachers of the early grades report that some of their students speak like much younger children. Although this is common, it presents a problem when teachers are not exactly sure what to do about it. Being reluctant to speak can be a normal developmental stage or a symptom of a communication disorder. Having trouble finding the right word in a discussion can be developmentally appropriate or a symptom of a deeper communication problem. "Sloppy" speech, "lazy" speech, and "confused" speech can be appropriate characteristics at one stage of development and symptoms of communication problems at another. Although failing to provide services when they are needed is a cause for concern, referring students for special education too early is also an appropriate professional concern. There are no easy answers.

Given the increasing diversity of school populations, most classroom teachers teach students from many cultures. The language systems used by these students is influenced by several factors, including geographic location, socioeconomic level, and ethnicity. Language differences must be addressed in classrooms. When does a difference in speaking patterns constitute a communication disorder? The concern is that some students enrolled in special education classes or who receive speech and language services may be inappropriately placed. Students may have no underlying communication problems but only culturally, regionally, or developmentally appropriate differences in their speech and language.

Imagine that you are placed in a German class with no knowledge or, at best, only a rudimentary knowledge of how to speak or read any foreign language. You are given an assignment to write an autobiography and present an oral report on it. You have been very successful in such activities in other settings. Your speaking and writing abilities are fine, but your first draft is unintelligible in any language. As a result of your clumsy and unacceptable skills, you are pulled out of the class and given a language test. Because of the poor results, you are placed in a special class to improve your language abilities. Your school career has been dramatically altered, perhaps inappropriately. Such a scenario is not as ridiculous as it may seem for students with dialectal differences. They may have been very effective communicators in their own cultures and may have learned language systems that were valued in those cultures. However, when the demands of a new educational experience require use of a new system, these students may be singled out and recommended for therapy.

In addition to differences in communication that arise from diverse student backgrounds, teachers will increasingly encounter students who have severe communication problems in any language. More and more, such students are being included in schools and programs with their neighbors and peers. Advances in technology have already made it possible for these individuals to compensate for most types of speech and language disorders. For example, personal computers can create synthetic speech to enable previously nonspeaking children to "talk" using a keyboard, communication board, or other input device. Some communication aids let users choose from a number of voices; alter the pitch and intensity of speech to convey emotions; and laugh, sing, and produce sound effects. In the not too distant future, the user of an electronic communication device may be able to design his or her own voice. These systems are constantly becoming more portable, less expensive, and better able to store vast numbers of words, sentences, and stories, enabling students with speech and language impairments to communicate more easily and effectively.

5

Communication Disorders in Perspective

The best-known story about a person with a speech disorder is that of the Greek orator and political leader, Demosthenes. He went down to the ocean, filled his mouth with pebbles, and shouted over the waves to cure his stuttering. In the 18th and 19th centuries, children with speech and language disorders usually were treated at clinics and hospitals. In 1908, the first public school class for students with speech disorders was established in New York. By 1910 the Chicago public schools were hiring "speech correction teachers," and by the early 1920s most large-city school systems had speech correction teachers on staff. In 1925, professionals in this field met and formed the American Academy of Speech Correction, known today as the American Speech-Language-Hearing Association (ASHA). A primary function of this organization is certification of professionals other than teachers who provide speech and language services.

TEAM APPROACH TO PROVIDING SERVICES

Most students with speech and language problems are found in general education classrooms. Until the early 1980s, it was common for speech-language pathologists to remove students from classrooms and give them brief periods of speech and language therapy in another setting. In the past few years, however, a shift from direct to indirect services has been more prominent. Increasingly, speech-language pathologists work with general and special education teachers to devise ways to facilitate speech and language development in their classrooms—for all their students, not just for those with speech or language problems.

Large numbers of students with communication problems put a load on the educational system and raise issues related to who receives special education and who is responsible for providing services. Some professionals argue that speech and language specialists should be responsible for identifying and treating all communication disorders. Specialized training and controlled instructional environments are cited as advantages of such a system of service delivery. Disadvantages cited are mostly related to assessment and interventions provided outside the general education classroom. As a result, some professionals support integrated models in which speech and language specialists are members of multidisciplinary intervention teams.

Who has the major responsibility for determining whether a difference in communication skills is due to a disorder or simply due to a language difference? Who is responsible for correcting speech and language problems? Who is best qualified to meet the needs of students with communication disorders? We believe that the most successful approach to helping students overcome speech and language challenges involves a joint effort of speech-language specialists, bilingual education teachers, and general education classroom teachers.

PULLING STUDENTS OUT
OF THE CLASSROOM

If students with speech or language problems receive services outside your classroom, work with the speech-language pathologist to identify the best time for each student to be gone. In general, it is better for students to be gone during independent practice time, their best subjects, or least favored class activities than during direct instructional times, subjects that require extra work, or favored activities. Try to keep a consistent schedule so students will know when to leave and what they will be missing each day. Provide cues (e.g., a clock with times marked on it), but have students assume responsibility for being on time for special services. When students return, have a system (such as an assignment buddy or work folder they can check) for getting them back with the regular program as quickly as possible. Recognize the need of each student with speech and language problems to receive special assistance, but try not to overgeneralize problems in other areas.

COMBATING NEGATIVE STEREOTYPES

Some of the terms used to describe students with communication disorders are listed in *Table 5.1*. Many of these terms have been used to describe students with other disabilities, and they tend to promote stereotyped thinking and negative impressions.

Table 5.1   Terms Used in Professional Literature to Describe Behaviors of Students with Speech & Language Problems

Aggressive	Impulsive
Anxious	Irritable
Asocial	Language delayed
Competitive	Language deviant
Confused	Language disordered
Daydreamer	Rigid
Developmentally aphasic	Shrewd
Disruptive	Shy
Distractible	Stubborn
Dysfluent	Submissive
Erratic	Unintelligent
Frustrated	Unmotivated
Immature	Uses baby talk

We include them as a reminder that, as with other types of disabilities, teachers and other professionals need to look carefully at the capabilities of students with speech and language problems, remembering the great diversity that can be hidden under a single label and the great disservice that can be done by lowering expectations.

TIPS TO IMPROVE COMMUNICATION

Communication takes place constantly and is involved in every activity of daily living. Speaking and listening are the most common ways we communicate, but communication disorders affect one in ten people in the United States (National Information Center, 2002). These impairments range from mild to severe difficulty in producing speech sounds, in fluency, and in producing or understanding language. Some people are unable to use speech at all. Regardless of where you work or what you do, you will encounter people with problems communicating. If you teach, some of these people will be your students. If you don't teach, some of these people will be your coworkers, neighbors, and peers. Because of the prevalence of speech and language difficulties, we end this section with a few suggestions for ways to improve communication:

If a student, colleague, neighbor, or friend has a communication disability, learn all you can about it and the ways to overcome it in your interactions.

Simplify information presented to people with communication disorders (e.g., speak slowly in a normal tone of voice, use short sentences, use rephrasing, and frequently check for understanding).

Present multiple forms of information.

Ask people with communication difficulties about their needs and ways you can overcome barriers to communication.

Show respect and sensitivity to individual differences and ask for help if you need it.

6

What Have We Learned?

A s you complete your study of teaching students with communication disorders, it may be helpful to review what you have learned. To help you check your understanding, we have listed the key points and key vocabulary for you to review. We have included the Self-Assessment again so you can compare what you know now with what you knew as you began your study. Finally, we provide a few topics for you to think about and some activities for you to do on your own.

Window on Practice:
The Work of a Speech-Language Specialist

My name is Lynn Wilcox, and I am a speech-language pathology supervisor in rural Nebraska. For approximately half of my time, I am responsible for the professional growth and evaluation of 15 persons who practice speech-language pathology and audiology in a county area. During the other half of my time, I attempt to provide consulting and diagnostic support to those clinicians and to other special education team members working with children from birth to age 21 for the communication problems associated with whatever disability conditions we identify.

(Continued)

(Continued)

I love my job. I love the people I work with and work for. Those feelings are not expressed lightly, nor should they imply that my job is in any way easy. I could tell you that I have great responsibility to see to it that child change occurs, but that would be an unfortunate exaggeration. Actually, I am a cheerleader. I am a politician. And I am a loving manager. I strive to be a fair, firm, and friendly evaluator. I attempt to be aware of resources, techniques, materials, programs, services, and on and on. Much more, though, it is my responsibility to be able to demonstrate and clearly explain to those I serve the areas I think the students need help in and what they can do to implement improvement. I am a one-on-one, inservice presenter who gets to coach the staff through a problem, direct their thinking a little, and enjoy watching their own excitement and the student's progress in relation to their efforts.

There are different supervisory styles. You may meet a supervisor along the way who functions differently from the way I do. My work is primarily directed toward the excitement of learning, and in that way I act primarily as a consultant to the clinician and very often to the resource teacher and the class teacher as well. I drop little nuggets about communication and how it affects class performance and test performance (particularly intelligence test performance) and offer suggestions about what can be done to support a student—in whatever setting—to anybody who will listen, either by mandate or by interest. I am not very good at sitting and watching someone work. I have discovered that the people with whom I work appreciate having me participate in activities and sessions with them. Observing is a viable supervisory style. I do it briefly sometimes, although usually my supervision occurs in action.

Sometimes I work as part of the team diagnosing a student's problem. I have to be able to clearly state what the problems are from a communication viewpoint. I have to make that information relevant to the classroom and particularly clear and relevant to the student's family. Then I either help write or provide ideas for writing educational plans that address the student's problems. I negotiate placement with administrators and other professionals who might see the problems differently than the way I see them. Sometimes I sit back while a clinician presents data and does the interpreting—oh, so important, that interpreting. Sometimes I am pleased because a clinician or a resource teacher or a parent really sees and understands how the student's communication fits into the scheme of things. Sometimes I am embarrassed by the lack of ability to interpret. I have to be careful not to wound clinicians and yet find a way to present uncomfortable information to them to make them want to learn instead of squashing their feelings just because I was embarrassed by their lack of preparation or information.

All in all, I spend about 50 or more hours every week doing something related to my profession. I am on call to each clinician at any time. In addition, I read, here and there, and call or write to those who replenish my own enthusiasm and my knowledge.

Maybe supervision can be done in a way that requires less dedication and less commitment. My personal philosophy is that I am willing to do more than I ask anyone else to do. I must be able to demonstrate any idea I present. I must understand my profession well enough to teach it to others.

Lynn Wilcox is a speech-language pathology supervisor from Hastings, Nebraska.

Bringing Learning to Life: John's Individualized Education Program Focuses on His Problems

After the school's diagnostic team determined that John's language problems were serious enough to justify special education, they prepared an individualized education program (IEP) to guide the delivery of these services. Following are selected components of John's IEP:

(Continued)

(Continued)

Annual Goals

1. By the end of the school year, John will use correct grammar in his spoken language 90 percent of the time. Person responsible: speech-language pathologist.

2. By the end of the school year, John will increase his spoken vocabulary score on the district language test from the 35th percentile to the 55th percentile. Person responsible: speech-language pathologist.

3. By the end of the school year, John will improve his use of articles, personal pronouns, adjectives, and proper verb tense to a level at least the same as 80 percent of his classroom peers. Person responsible: classroom teacher (using specifically prepared lessons with assistance from speech-language pathologist).

General Education Class Participation

John will spend instructional time for all academic subjects in the general education class.

Related Services

1. John will receive special education services from a speech-language pathologist for 30 minutes every other day.

2. John's teacher will be provided with consultation from the speech-language pathologist on a weekly basis and as needed.

KEY POINTS

▣ Communication disorders related to speech and language are the second most common reason students receive special education.

◙ Speech disorders include problems producing speech sounds (articulation disorders), controlling sounds that are produced (voice disorders), and controlling the rate and rhythm of speech (fluency disorders).

◙ Language problems include difficulties using proper forms of language (phonology, morphology, syntax), using the context of language (semantics), and using the functions of language (pragmatics).

◙ Students with communication disorders often receive special education from speech-language pathologists, but sometimes people disagree about the relative responsibilities of these professionals and classroom teachers.

◙ General interventions for communication disorders include providing good models, an accepting classroom environment, and practice developing newly acquired speech skills.

◙ A continuing concern for teachers is differentiating true communication problems from cultural or dialectal language differences.

KEY VOCABULARY

Articulation disorder is the abnormal production of speech sounds.

Communication disorders are a special education category that includes students whose problems producing speech or using language symbols interfere significantly with their ability to communicate.

Expressive language refers to the production of language.

Fluency disorder is the abnormal flow of verbal expression, characterized by impaired rate and rhythm, which may be accompanied by struggle behavior.

Grammar refers to the structure of language; it can be the root of a language problem.

Language disorders include problems with using proper forms of language (phonology, morphology, syntax), using the content of language (semantics), and using the functions of language (pragmatics).

Language evaluation includes formal and informal tests used to gather information about the seriousness of language problems.

Morphology is concerned with the smallest units of meaningful language (morphemes or words and parts of words).

Phonology is concerned with the smallest units of language (phonemes or speech sounds).

Pragmatics is concerned with the use and function of language in varying settings.

Receptive language refers to hearing, listening to, or receiving language.

Semantics is concerned with word and message meanings (vocabulary, comprehension, following directions).

Speech disorders include problems producing speech sounds (articulation), controlling sounds that are produced (voice), and controlling the rate and rhythm of speech (fluency).

Speech evaluation consists of gathering information about the seriousness of speech problems, often in the form of a series of checklists.

Speech-language pathologist is a professional who provides special education services for students with communication disorders and works with teachers to enhance instruction in language.

Vocabulary refers to understanding the meaning of words; it can be the root of a language problem.

Voice disorder is the absence or abnormal production of vocal quality, pitch, loudness, resonance, and/or duration.

Written expression refers to communication through written language.

Self-Assessment 2

A fter you complete this book, check your knowledge and understanding of the content covered. Choose the best answer for each of the following questions.

1. The two main types of communication disorders are

   a. Speech disorders and articulation problems

   b. Speech disorders and language disorders

   c. Receptive language disorders and expressive language disorders

   d. Written expression disorders and expressive language disorders

2. The absence or abnormal production of vocal quality, pitch, loudness, resonance, or duration is known as a (or an)

   a. Articulation disorder

   b. Fluency disorder

   c. Morphology disorder

   d. Voice disorder

3. Which of the following is NOT related to language disorders?

   a. Articulation

   b. Function

   c. Form

   d. Content

4. When a student is unable to identify appropriate pictures when word names are provided, that student might have difficulty with

    a. Morphology

    b. Pragmatics

    c. Semantics

    d. Syntax

5. The caseload of a speech-language pathologist consists primarily of students who receive services for _____ or _____ disorders.

    a. Morphology, phonology

    b. Receptive, expressive

    c. Articulation, fluency

    d. Articulation, language

6. The most common fluency disorder is

    a. Slow speech

    b. Stuttering

    c. Inappropriate repetition

    d. Self-interruption

7. The most common accepted term for a communication disorders professional is

    a. Speech-language pathologist

    b. Teachers of the speech and language impaired

    c. Speech therapist

    d. Speech correction teacher

8. Which of the following is NOT an appropriate suggestion for teachers working with students with communication disorders?

   a. Use areas of strength to compensate for weakness.

   b. Provide good speech models.

   c. Tell students to "take their time" when they stutter.

   d. Value speech and language diversity.

9. To improve the use of grammar, teachers should focus on

   a. Sentence structure

   b. Expressive language

   c. Pronunciation

   d. Meaning

10. A teacher completes a series of checklists concerning Sara's speech patterns, and the speech-language pathologist talks informally with Sara. These steps are part of the _____ process.

   a. Special education

   b. Referral

   c. Evaluation

   d. Information

11. The Peabody is a test of

   a. Language comprehension

   b. Articulation

   c. Phonology

   d. Vocabulary

12. Which of the following is a tactic for helping students to overcome social and emotional problems?

    a. Convey information with praise.

    b. Be careful to praise, not embarrass, students.

    c. Praise the obvious.

    d. All of the above.

13. Which of the following should be taken into account when deciding whether a student needs special education for communication difficulties?

    a. Intelligence

    b. Cultural differences

    c. Behavior problems

    d. Grades

14. The organization for communication disorders professionals is the

    a. American Academy of Speech Correction

    b. National Association of Communication Disorders

    c. Speech and Language Association of America

    d. American Speech-Language-Hearing Association

15. Students who are pulled out of their classrooms for speech or language services should be pulled out during

    a. Independent practice time

    b. Favorite subjects

    c. Core courses

    d. None of the above

16. Which of the following is an appropriate word for describing a student with communication disorders?

    a. Language disordered

    b. Language delayed

    c. Language deviant

    d. None of the above

REFLECTION

After you answer the multiple-choice questions, provide a short answer to the following questions:

- In what areas are students with communication disorders likely to experience difficulties?
- What is the difference between language and speech disorders, and which is more common?
- What is your opinion regarding the delivery of speech and language services—should they be conducted in the classroom or in a special education setting?

Answer Key for Self-Assessments

1. b

2. d

3. a

4. c

5. d

6. b

7. a

8. c

9. d

10. c

11. d

12.   d

13.   b

14.   d

15.   a

16.   d

On Your Own

☑ Volunteer to work in a setting where people with communication disorders are provided services. Participate for at least two hours on five occasions. Describe the jobs you were given. Describe assistance you were provided by professionals working at the setting. Describe how you would organize a volunteer experience if you were working in the same setting.

☑ Draw a diagram illustrating how the following words or phrases are related to each other: articulation, communication, content, expressive, fluency, form, function, grammar, language, pragmatics, receptive, semantics, speech, syntax, and voice. Write a short paragraph that describes the diagram.

☑ Ask a teacher of a student with a speech problem to share his or her instructional approaches.

☑ Interview three professionals who work with people with communication disorders in three different settings. Ask them to describe what they do and any special methods they use to improve speech or language skills.

☑ Select a journal that focuses on students with communication disorders (see Resources). Browse the most recent issues in your library. Note the types of articles that are included (such as research, opinion, practical suggestions). Find at least three articles that describe specific teaching activities you could used to improve speech problems. Find at least three articles that describe specific teaching activities you could use to improve language problems.

Resources

BOOKS

Leonard, L. B. (1999). *Children with specific language impairment.* Cambridge: MIT Press. This comprehensive overview of language impairments discusses the history of these impairments, possible biological origins, and clinical and educational practices.

JOURNALS AND ARTICLES

ASHA Journal. Published by the American Speech-Language-Hearing Association (ASHA), this journal pertains to the professional and administrative activities of speech-language pathology, audiology, and ASHA. It includes articles, special reports, news items, committee reports, reviews of books and materials, and letters. Articles are of broad professional interest and may be philosophical, conceptual, historical, or synthesizing. ASHA, 10801 Rockville Pike, Rockville, MD 20852–3279.

Journal of Speech and Hearing Disorders (JSHD). JSHD is intended for professionals interested in disordered speech, language, and hearing, particularly clinicians who provide services to people with communication disorders and researchers who study the causes, assessment, and treatment of speech and language disorders. Terry L. Wiley, Editor, JSHD, University of Wisconsin-Madison, Department of Communication Disorders, 1975 Willow Dr., Madison, WI 53706.

Journal of Speech and Hearing Research (JSHR). This publication of ASHA pertains broadly to studies of the process and disorders of speech, hearing, and language. It includes experimental reports; theoretical, tutorial, or review papers; brief research notes describing clinical procedures or instruments; and letters to the editor. John H. Saxman, Coordinating Editor, JSHR, Box 146, Teachers College, Columbia University, New York, NY 10027.

Language, Speech, and Hearing Services in the Schools (LSHSS). This ASHA journal pertains to speech, hearing, and language services for children, particularly in schools. Articles deal with all aspects of clinical services to children, including the nature, assessment, and remediation of speech, hearing, and language disorders; program organization; management and supervision; and scholarly discussion of philosophical issues relating to school programming. Wayne A. Secord, Editor, LSHSS, Ohio State University, 110 Pressy Hall, 1070 Carmack Rd., Columbus, OH 43210–1002.

ORGANIZATIONS

American Speech-Language-Hearing Association (ASHA)

ASHA is the primary organization that supports families, children, and educational programs for individuals with communication disorders. It promotes awareness and supportive activities, as well as preparation standards and competencies for speech-language pathologists. Members must hold a master's degree or equivalent with emphasis in speech-language pathology, audiology, or speech and hearing science or a master's degree or equivalent and present evidence of active research, interest, and performance in the field of human communication. ASHA, 10801 Rockville Pike, Rockville, MD 20852–3276.

Division for Children With Communication Disorders (DCCD)

A division of the Council for Exceptional Children, DCCD encourages membership of professionals interested in program development and preparation activities related to students with communication disorders. DCCD provides outlets for the exchange of ideas through a variety of resources, including special publications and annual conferences. CEC, 1100 North Glebe Road, Arlington, VA 22201–5704.

International Society for Augmentative and Alternative Communication (ISAAC)

ISSAC is devoted to enhancing the education, employment, and daily living of people with communication disorders. It produces a journal, *Augmentative and Alternative Communication,* and a newsletter; it also sponsors a biennial conference. ISAAC, P.O. Box 1762, Station R, Toronto, Ontario, Canada M4G 4A3.

References

American Speech-Language-Hearing Association. (1982). Definitions: Communicative disorders and variations. *ASHA, 24,* 949–950.

American Speech-Language-Hearing Association. (1993). Definitions: Communication disorders and variations. *ASHA, 35* (Suppl. 10) 40–41.

Carrow-Woolfolk, E. (1999). *Test for auditory comprehension of language* (3rd ed.). Austin, TX: Pro-Ed.

Dunn, Lloyd M., & Dunn, Leota M. (2000). *Peabody picture vocabulary test-revised.* Palo Alto, CA: CPP.

Foster, R., Giddan, J. J., & Stark, J. (1983). *Assessment of children's language comprehension.* Palo Alto, CA: CPP.

Goldman, R., & Fristoe, M. (2000). *Goldman-Fristoe test of articulation* (2nd ed.). Circle Pines, MN: American Guidance Service.

Lewis, R. B., & Doorlag, D. H. (1991). *Teaching special students in the mainstream* (3rd ed.). Columbus, OH: Merrill.

Mizuko, M. (2002). *Who is likely to stutter?* Unpublished manuscript. Duluth: University of Minnesota.

National Information Center for Children and Youths With Disabilities. (2002). *Communication disorders fact sheet.* Retrieved December 26, 2005, from http://www.nichcy.org

Index

Note: Numbers in **Bold** followed by a colon [:] denote the book number within which the page numbers are found.

AAMR (American Association on
    Mental Retardation), **12:**6,
    12:20–21, **12:**66
Ability training,
    4:39–40, **4:**62
Academic achievement, assessing,
    3:37–39
    achievement tests, **3:**37, **3:**77
    interviews, **3:**38–39
    observations, **3:**38
    portfolios, **3:**39
Academic engaged time,
    3:22–23, **3:**76
Academic learning disabilities, **9:**51
Academic time analysis,
    3:22–23, **3:**76
Acceleration or advancement,
    13:25–27, **13:**36–40, **13:**52
Acceptability, **3:**56–57
Accommodations
    defining, **3:**77
    for student with sensory
        disabilities, **7:**49–51
    in general education classrooms,
        1:21–22
    without patronization, **4:**14
    See also Instruction, adapting for
        students with
        special needs

Accountability, **3:**17, **3:**77
    outcomes-based, **3:**23, **6:**35
Acculturation, **3:**63, **3:**77
Achievement tests, **3:**37, **3:**77
Acting out, **3:**47
Active observation, **3:**29, **3:**77
Adams, C. M., **1:**35–36
Adaptive behavior, **3:**41–43, **3:**77
    defining, **12:**21
    environmental effects on, **3:**42–43
    mental retardation and, **12:**17,
        12:19–25, **12:**21 (tab)–23
        (tab), **12:**45–49
Adaptive behavior scales,
    3:42, **12:**71
Adaptive devices, **8:**52, **8:**62–63
ADHD. *See* Attention deficit
    hyperactivity disorder
Adult literacy/lifelong learning,
    5:50, **6:**27–28
Advanced Placement (AP), **13:**26
Advocacy groups, **6:**11,
    6:12–13, **6:**44
Ahlgren, C., **12:**67
AIDS, **5:**10, **8:**12–13, **8:**58–59, **8:**63
Aim line, **4:**29, **4:**63
Alcohol-/drug-free schools, **6:**28–29
Algozzine, B., **4:**5, **6:**9, **12:**62
Alley, G., **4:**45

Allocation of funds,
6:15, 6:16–17, 6:44
Allsop, J., 8:49
Alternative living unit (ALU),
5:31, 5:54
Alternative-print format, 3:71
Alternatives for recording
answers, 3:71
Amendments to the Education for
All Handicapped Children Act,
2:11 (tab)
Amendments to the Individuals
With Disabilities Education
Act, 2:12 (tab), 2:27–29
American Association on Mental
Retardation (AAMR),
12:6, 12:11, 12:18–19,
12:20–21, 12:66
American Asylum for the
Education and Instruction
of the Deaf, 2:9–10
American Federation
of Teachers, 6:11
American Psychiatric
Association, 9:44
American Sign Language (ASL),
7:40, 7:59
American Speech-Language-
Hearing Association
(ASHA), 10:10, 10:35
Americans With Disabilities
Act (ADA), 2:12 (tab),
2:26–27, 2:54, 8:49
Amplification systems, 4:51, 7:41
Analysis error, 3:38, 3:78
Analytical programs, 9:27, 9:56
Antia, S. D., 7:26
Anxiety, 11:18–22, 11:46
AP (Advanced Placement), 13:26
Apprenticeships programs,
5:45, 5:56
Appropriate education,
2:42 (tab), 2:46, 2:54
ARC (Association for Retarded
Citizens), 12:66
Architectural accessibility, 2:14, 2:54
Articulation disorder,
10:9–10, 10:43

Asch, A., 7:33–34
ASHA (American
Speech-Language-Hearing
Association), 10:10, 10:35
Assessment
academic achievement, 3:37–39
alternatives for recording
answers, 3:71
classroom, 3:73–74
curriculum-based,
3:19–21, 3:78, 9:19
data collection for, 3:25–31
defining, 3:77
ecobehavioral, 3:22–23, 3:78
effects of, 3:74
error and, 3:62–63
formal, 3:11
functional academic,
9:19, 9:57
functional behavioral, 9:19, 9:57,
11:15–16, 11:47
instructional environments,
3:23, 3:77
needs, 4:41, 4:64
portfolios, 3:26, 3:39, 3:80
prereferral interventions, 3:11
psychoeducational, 3:9, 3:81
psychological development,
3:45–47
skilled examiner for, 3:59–61
work-sample, 3:26, 3:81
See also Assessment guidelines;
Assessment practices; Data
collection; Protection in
evaluation procedures
Assessment,
decision-making and
accountability, 3:17
child-study team role in, 3:12–15
eligibility/entitlement, 3:14–15
exceptionality decisions, 3:12
instructional planning, 3:15
intervention assistance, 3:10
overview of, 3:8 (tab)
program evaluation, 3:16–17
progress evaluation, 3:15–16
psychoeducational assessment
referral, 3:9

screening decisions, **3**:7–10
special help/enrichment, **3**:10
special learning needs, **3**:13–14
Assessment guidelines, **3**:65–71
    accommodation, **3**:71
    environment, **3**:70–71
    frequency, **3**:69
    improving instruction, **3**:69
    more than describing
        problems, **3**:67–69
    no one cause of school
        problems, **3**:66
    no right way to assess, **3**:66
    variables, **3**:70
Assessment practices, **3**:17–24
    curriculum-based assessment,
        3:19–21
    curriculum-based measurement,
        3:21–22
    instructional diagnosis, **3**:22
    instructional
        environments, **3**:23
    outcomes-based accountability,
        3:23
    performance assessment, **3**:24
    See also Reliability;
        Representativeness; Validity
Assisted listening devices,
    7:39 (tab), **7**:41, **7**:42
Assistive technologies,
    2:26, **7**:13, **7**:52
Association for Retarded Citizens
    (ARC), **12**:66
Asthma, **8**:9–10, **8**:11 (tab), **8**:63
Astigmatism, **7**:10, **7**:59
At risk student, **2**:24, **3**:8, **3**:9,
    5:14–15, **6**:20, **13**:14
Ataxic cerebral palsy, **8**:24
Athetoid cerebral palsy, **8**:24
Attack strategy training,
    4:40, **4**:63
Attention deficit
    hyperactivity disorder
        (ADHD), **2**:15, **8**:34
    criteria for, **9**:44 (tab)–45 (tab)
    defining, **9**:43–46, **9**:56
    remediating, **9**:46–48
Audio aids, **7**:36 (tab)

Audiometer, **3**:40, **3**:77
Auditory acuity, **7**:19, **7**:59
Autism, **1**:15–16, **1**:40, **8**:17,
    8:28–31, **8**:63
Automaticity, **4**:20, **4**:63
Auxiliary aids, **2**:14

Bain, J. D., **4**:5
Barnett, S., **5**:16
Barraga, N. C., **7**:8
Basic skills, **9**:56
Batshaw, M. L., **8**:22, **8**:47
Beattie v. State Board of Education,
    2:36 (tab)
Behavior intervention plan, **11**:16,
    11:46
Behavior therapy, **4**:38, **4**:63
Bennett, T., **3**:21
Berdine, W. H., **8**:46
Berrueta-Clement, J., **5**:16
Biklen, D., **6**:41
Bingo (game), **12**:40 (fig)
Blackhurst, A. E., **8**:46
Blackorby, J., **5**:24
Bland, L. C., **1**:35–36
Blindisms, **7**:14
Blindness, **1**:16
    defining, **1**:40, **7**:8–9, **7**:59
    See also Braille; Visual
        impairments
Bloom, B., **4**:41
Books (resources)
    assessment, **3**:91–92
    communication
        disorders, **10**:57
    effective instruction, **4**:75–76
    emotional disturbance, **11**:57–60
    fundamentals of special
        education, **1**:53
    gifted and talented child,
        13:63–64
    learning disabilities, **9**:67
    legal foundations, **2**:65–66
    medical/physical/multiple
        disabilities, **8**:75–80
    mental retardation, **12**:81–84
    public policy/school
        reform, **6**:55

sensory disabilities, **7:**73–77
transitions, **5:**65–67
Bounty hunting, **6:**17
Braille, **4:**52, **7:**10, **7:**13, **7:**15, **7:**16,
    7:34, **7:**35 (tab)
Braille display technology,
    7:37, **7:**59
Braille note-taking devices, **7:**38
Braille printers, **7:**37, **7:**59
Brailler, **4:**52, **4:**63
Brooks-Gunn, J., **5:**15
Brophy, J., **4:**13
Brown, F., **3:**62–63
Brown, L., **12:**55, **12:**67
Brown v. Board of Education,
    2:35, **2:**36 (tab), **2:**44
Bryant, B., **3:**37
Bureau of Indian Affairs,
    6:11, **6:**13
Burlington School Committee
    v. Massachusetts Board of
    Education, **2:**42 (tab), **2:**46–47
Byrnes, L. J., **7:**26

Callahan, C. M., **1:**35–36
Cameto, R., **5:**24
Cancer, **8:**11 (tab), **8:**63
Canes, for students with visual
    impairments, **4:**55
Carrow-Woolfolk, E., **10:**26
Carta, J., **3:**22, **4:**46
Carter, K., **7:**38
Cartwright, C., **4:**53
Cartwright, G., **4:**53
Case, L. P., **9:**17–18
Categorical programs,
    1:17, **6:**16, **6:**44
CCTV (closed-circuit television),
    7:35 (tab), **7:**36–37
CEC (Council for Exceptional
    Children), **12:**66
Cefalu v. East Baton Rouge
    Parish School Board,
    2:43 (tab)–44 (tab)
Center-based programs,
    5:13, **5:**14, **5:**54
Cerebral palsy, **8:**23–24, **8:**63
CHADD, **9:**46

Chadsey-Rusch, J., **5:**24
Chalfant, J. C., **9:**51
Chang, S. C., **7:**15
Child-find programs,
    7:30, **7:**59
Child-study team, **3:**12–15, **3:**77
Choate, J., **3:**21
Christenson, S. L., **3:**14, **3:**23
Citizens Concerned About
    Disability, **6:**11
Civil Rights Act, **2:**26
Clark, B., **4:**41
Classification
    changes in practices, **6:**8–9
    defining, **6:**44
Classroom amplification systems,
    7:41, **7:**51
Classroom assessment, **3:**73–74
Classwide peer tutoring,
    4:47, **4:**63
Client-centered therapy,
    4:43–44, **4:**63
Cloninger, C., **12:**59
Close-captioned television, **4:**51
Closed-circuit television (CCTV),
    7:35 (tab), **7:**36–37
Coefficient, reliability, **3:**50, **3:**81
Cognitive behavior modification,
    4:41, **4:**63
Cognitive mapping, **7:**34
Cognitive skills training,
    4:41, **4:**43
Cohen, H. J., **8:**13
Coleman, M. C., **11:**36
Coleman, M. R., **13:**11, **13:**45
Committee for Economic
    Development, **5:**14–15
Communication boards,
    4:50, **8:**41, **8:**63
Communication disorders
    academic characteristics
        of, **10:**14
    behavioral characteristics
        of, **10:**15
    cognitive characteristics
        of, **10:**13–14
    combating negative stereotypes
        about, **10:**37 (tab)–38

communication characteristics
of, **10:**15–16
defining, **10:**43
fluency problems, **10:**16
identifying, **10:**24–27
language disorders, **10:**10–11
language problems, **10:**16
phonology/morphology/
syntax problems, **10:**10–11
physical characteristics of,
10:14–15
pragmatics problems, **10:**11
pulling students from classroom,
10:36–37
semantics problems, **10:**11
speech disorders, **10:**9–10
team approach to providing
services, **10:**35–36
tips to improve communication,
10:38
voice problems, **10:**15
See also Communication
disorders, teaching
students with
Communication disorders, teaching
students with, **10:**17–30
interpersonal problems, **10:**27–30
language problems, **10:**20–27
speech problems, **10:**18–20
tips for teachers, **10:**19 (tab)
trends/issues influencing,
10:31–33
Communication skills, **3:**42
Communication/motility. *See*
Instructional adaptations, to
increase
Community collaboration,
5:7, **5:**43–46, **5:**55, **13:**48
Compensatory education,
3:10, **3:**77
Competitive employment,
5:24–25, **5:**55
Computer-assisted
instruction, **4:**5
Concentration game, **12:**41 (fig)
Concussion, **8:**25–26, **8:**63
Conductive hearing loss,
7:19, **7:**59

Conlon, C. J., **8:**14
Consultative (indirect) services,
1:26, **1:**40, **1:**41, **5:**12, **5:**55
Contextual variables, **4:**10, **4:**63
Continued education, **5:**26–27
Contusions, **8:**26, **8:**63
Convergent thinking,
13:17–18, **13:**52
Cooperative learning,
4:45–46, **4:**63
Corn, A., **7:**15
Corrective/supportive feedback,
4:40, **4:**46–47, **12:**37, **12:**43
Council for Children With
Behavioral Disorders, **11:**36
Council for Exceptional Children
(CEC), **12:**66
Counseling therapy,
4:43–45, **4:**63
*Covarrubias v. San Diego Unified
School District*, **2:**38 (tab)
Craniofacial anomalies,
8:22, **8:**63
Creative ability, **1:**34, **1:**40–41
Creative-productive giftedness,
13:43, **13:**52
Creech, B., **7:**26, **7:**42
Crisis therapy, **4:**44–45, **4:**63
Criterion-referenced tests, **3:**28–29,
3:77–78, **4:**9, **4:**64
Critical thinking, **4:**43
Crittenden, J. B., **7:**87
Crocker, A. C., **8:**13
Cued speech, **7:**39 (tab),
7:40–41, **7:**42
Cues
auditory, **7:**16, **7:**28, **7:**43
defining, **9:**56
phonetic, **9:**29, **9:**57
to improve math, **9:**32
to improve work
habits, **9:**36
to reduce behavior problems,
10:37, **11:**24
Curriculum compacting,
13:39, **13:**40
Curriculum-based assessment,
3:19–21, **3:**78, **9:**19

Curriculum-based measurement,
   3:21–22, **3:**78
Curriculum-referenced tests. *See*
   Criterion-referenced tests
Currie, J., **5:**15
Cystic fibrosis, **8:**12, **8:**63

D'Allura, T., **7:**14
D'Amico, R., **5:**24
Data collection, for assessments,
   3:25–31
Davidson, J. E., **13:**43
Davis, L., **12:**67
Deaf
   defining, **7:**18, **7:**21, **7:**59
   See also Deaf-and-blind/
      deaf-blind; Hearing
      impairments
Deaf culture, **7:**26, **7:**59
Deaf-and-blind/deaf-blind
   characteristics of, **7:**31–32
   defining, **7:**29–30, **7:**59–60
   prevalence of, **7:**30
Deafness and blindness,
   1:16, **1:**41, **7:**6, **7:**60
Deafness or hearing impairment,
   1:16, **1:**41
Deinstitutionalization,
   5:30, **5:**55
Delquadri, J., **4:**46
Dennis, R., **12:**59
Deno, S. L., **3:**22
Denton, P., **4:**45
Deshler, D., **4:**45
Developmental learning
   disabilities, **9:**51
Diabetes, **8:**11 (tab), **8:**63
Diagnostic tests, **3:**28, **3:**78
*Diana v. State Board of
   Education*, **2:**37 (tab)
Direct instruction,
   principles of, **4:**64
   corrective/supportive feedback,
      4:40, **4:**46–47, **12:**37, **12:**43
   independent practice,
      4:40, **10:**36–37
   modeling expected
      behavior, **4:**40

task analysis, **3:**22, **3:**81,
   4:10, **4:**40, **4:**65,
   12:43–45, **12:**72
   See also Instruction
Direct services, **1:**25, **1:**41, **5:**12, **5:**55
Discrepancy
   defining, **9:**56
   dual, **9:**17–18
   eliminating, **9:**9
Discrepant scores, **3:**34, **3:**78, **12:**30
Discrimination, protection
   against, **1:**13
Distractibility (nonattention),
   3:47, **11:**47
Disturbed peer relations, **3:**47
Divergent thinking, **13:**17, **13:**52
Diverse students, **1:**29–31
Doorlag, D. H., **10:**18–20
Down syndrome, **12:**13–14,
   12:66, **12:**71
Drop out rate, **1:**30–31
Drug addiction, pregnancy
   and, **5:**10, **8:**14–15
DSM-IV, **9:**45 (tab)
Dual discrepancy, **9:**17–18
Due process, **1:**13, **1:**41, **2:**21,
   2:54, **2:**55
Duhaime, A., **8:**25, **8:**26, **8:**27
Dunn, Leota M., **10:**27
Dunn, Lloyd M., **10:**27
Duration recording, **3:**46, **3:**78

Early intervention
   as part of lifelong
      learning, **5:**50
   defining, **2:**55, **5:**55, **6:**44
   direct/indirect services for, **5:**12
   effectiveness of, **5:**14–16
   federal laws/incentives
      for, **5:**11–12
   for infants/toddlers, **2:**24
   Head Start, **5:**15
   home-based programs, **5:**12–13
   hospital-/center-based programs,
      5:13–14
   need for more programs, **5:**10
   preschool, **5:**9–10
   social factor influence on, **6:**9–10

special education services,
   5:10–11 (fig)
Ypsilanti Perry Preschool
   Project, **5:**15–16
E-books, **9:**29
Echolalia, **8:**41, **11:**14
Ecobehavioral assessment,
   3:22–23, **3:**78
Edelman, S., **12:**59
Education, defining, **1:**9, **1:**41
Education for All Handicapped
   Children Act, **1:**12;
   2:11 (tab), **1:**19
   amendments to, **2:**24–25, **2:**48–49
   defining, **2:**56
   early childhood education and,
      5:11–12
   objectives of, **2:**15
   problems addressed by, **2:**15–16
   provisions of
      (*See* Individualized
      education programs; Least
      restrictive environment;
      Protection in evaluation
      procedures)
   specific learning disabilities and,
      9:11–12
   specific procedures of, **2:**16
   See also Individuals With
      Disabilities Education Act
Educational settings
   diverse, **1:**31–32
   variations by state, **1:**32
   See also Least restrictive
      environment
Egel, A. L., **8:**30
Ekwall, E., **3:**38
Electronic travel aids, **4:**55–56, **4:**64
Elementary and Secondary
   Education Act (ESEA). *See*
   No Child Left Behind Act
Eligibility decisions, **1:**22, **3:**14–15,
   3:78, **7:**9–10, **7:**55
Elliott, J., **4:**5
Emotional disturbance
   academic characteristics of,
      11:10–11
   anxiety, **11:**18–22

behavior intervention plans,
      11:15–16
   behavioral characteristics of,
      11:12–14
   cognitive characteristics of,
      11:9–10
   communication characteristics
      of, **11:**14
   defining, **1:**16, **1:**41, **11:**7–9,
      11:35–37, **11:**39–40
   functional behavioral assessment
      and, **11:**15–16
   improving social interactions,
      11:13–14
   medical treatment for, **11:**37–38
   physical characteristics of,
      11:11–12
   psychosomatic, **11:**11
   terms used to describe,
      11:10 (tab)
   See also Emotional disturbance,
      teaching students with
Emotional disturbance, teaching
   students with
   anxiety, **11:**18–22
   behavior intervention plans,
      11:17–26
   disruptiveness, **11:**27–29
   nonattention (distractibility),
      11:29–30
   school opposition/
      noncompliance, **11:**23 (tab)
   social problems, **11:**27–33
   task avoidance, **11:**31–33
   temper tantrums, **11:**24–26
   tips for school opposition/
      noncompliance, **11:**23 (tab)
   tips for school phobia, **11:**21 (tips)
   tips for teachers of, **11:**18 (tab)
   tips for temper tantrums,
      11:25–26
   tips for test-taking, **11:**22 (tab)
   trends/issues influencing,
      11:35–37
Emotional problems, **11:**17, **11:**47
Employment, sheltered/ supported,
   5:25, **5:**56
Empowerment movement, **7:**47

Enhanced image devices,
    7:36–37, **7:**60
Enrichment, **3:**10, **3:**78,
    13:23–24, **13:**28–36, **13:**53
Enright, B., **3:**21
Entwistle, D., **4:**5
Entwistle, N., **4:**5
Epidural hematomas, **8:**26, **8:**64
Epilepsy, **8:**23, **8:**64
Epilepsy Foundation
    of America, **8:**47
Epstein, A., **5:**16
Epstein, J. L.
Equal access, **2:**14, **2:**41 (tab), 45–46
Equal protection clause,
    2:7–8, **2:**53, **2:**55
ERIC Clearinghouse on Disabilities
    and Gifted Education, **1:**11
Erin, J. N., **7:**8
Error analysis, **3:**38, **3:**78
Errors
    assessment, **3:**62–63
    halo effect, **3:**62
    integration, **3:**48
    logical, **3:**62
    of central tendency, **3:**62
    of leniency, **3:**62
    perseveration, **3:**38, **3:**48
    rotation, **3:**48
    sensitivity, **3:**62
Errors of central tendency, **3:**62
Errors of leniency, **3:**62
Ethell, R. G., **4:**5
Evaluation
    defining, **4:**64
    formative, **4:**23, **4:**64
    language, **10:**44
    process, **1:**24
    program, **3:**16–17, **3:**80
    progress, **1:**24, **3:**80
    protection in procedures,
        1:13, **1:**42, **2:**21–23, **2:**56
    speech, **10:**44
    summative, **4:**23, **4:**65
Event recording, **3:**46, **3:**78
Exceptional students, defining, **1:**41
Exceptionality decisions,
    3:12, **3:**78–79

Exclusion, **2:**19 (fig),
    2:42 (tab), **2:**49–50
Expressive language, **10:**43

Face validity, **3:**57, **3:**79
Families/community agencies. *See*
    Community collaboration;
    Early intervention; Family
    involvement; Transition
    services
Family involvement, **5:**7
    adverse affects of disability on
        family, **5:**38
    affect of exceptionalities on
        families, **5:**35–37
    gifted student concerns, **5:**37–38
    home–school
        collaboration barriers, **5:**41
        (tab)–42 (tab)
    home–school collaboration
        barriers, overcoming,
        5:39–40, **5:**42
    institutionalization *vs.* home care
        issues, **5:**38
    types of, **5:**39
    with communication disorders,
        10:30
FAPE (free and appropriate
    education), **2:**55
Fazzi, D. L., **7:**7, **7:**11
Feedback
    auditory, **7:**37
    corrective/supportive, **4:**46–47,
        12:37, **12:**43
    defining, **4:**21, **4:**64
    tactile, **7:**31
Fetal alcohol syndrome,
    5:10, **8:**14, **8:**64
Finger spelling, **7:**40, **7:**60
Flexible promotion, **13:**25
Flexible scheduling,
    3:71, **4:**54, **4:**64
Flexible settings, **3:**71, **4:**54, **4:**64
Fluency disorder, **10:**10, **10:**43
Forlenza-Bailey, A., **4:**5
Formal assessments, **3:**11
Formal interviews, **3:**30
Formal observations, **3:**27, **3:**29

Formal tests, **3:**27, **3:**79
Formative evaluation, **4:**23, **4:**64
Forster, G., **6:**53
Foster, R., **10:**27
Foster homes, **5:**31–32
Frederick L. v. Thomas,
 2:39 (tab)–40 (tab)
Free and appropriate education
 (FAPE), **2:**55
Frequency, **7:**20 (tab), **7:**60
Fristoe, M., **10:**26
Fuchs, D., **9:**17
Full inclusion, **6:**21
Functional academic assessment,
 9:19, **9:**57
Functional behavioral assessment,
 9:19, **9:**57, **11:**15–16, **11:**47
Functional hearing losses, **7:**24, **7:**25
 (tab), **7:**60
Funding, **6:**15, **6:**16–17, **6:**44

Gallagher, J., **13:**11,
 13:19, **13:**20, **13:**45
Gallaudet Research Institute
 (GRI), **7:**22
Gallup, A. M., **11:**39
Gardner, H., **13:**43
Giangreco, M. F., **12:**59
Gickling, E., **3:**20
Giddan, J. J., **10:**27
Gifted, defining, **13:**53
Gifted and Talented Children's
 Education Act, **1:**33–34,
 13:10–11
Gifted and talented students
 academic characteristics of,
  13:18–19
 behavioral characteristics of,
  13:20–21
 characteristics of,
  13:15–22, **13:**16 (tab)–17 (tab)
 cognitive characteristics of,
  13:15–18
 communication characteristics of,
  13:21–22
 concerns of families with,
  5:37–38
 creative ability, **1:**34, **1:**40

creative-productive giftedness,
  13:43
 criteria other than intelligence
  test to determine, **13:**42–43
 defining, **1:**16, **1:**41
 evolving concept of giftedness,
  13:41–42
 federal legislation concerning,
  13:9–11
 identifying gifts/talents, **1:**35–36
 identifying students as, **13:**12–14
 intellectual ability of, **1:**34
 leadership ability of, **1:**35
 physical characteristics of,
  13:19–20
 schoolhouse
  giftedness, **13:**43
 specific academic ability, **1:**34–35
 state definitions of, **13:**11–12
 terms used to describe,
  13:10 (tab)
 underrepresented groups in
  category of, **13:**44–45
 visual/performing arts ability of,
  1:35, **1:**40
 See also Gifted and talented
  students, teaching
Gifted and talented students,
 teaching
 acceleration tactics, **13:**36–40
 acceleration/advancement
  approach, **13:**25–27
 criteria other than intelligence
  test, **13:**42–43
 enrichment approach, **13:**23–24
 enrichment tactics, **13:**28–36
 extending knowledge in content
  areas, **13:**31–33
 extending knowledge into new
  areas, **13:**33–36 (fig)
 practicing/polishing skills,
  13:28–31 (fig)
 teacher tips, **13:**24 (tab), **13:**45–46
 trends/issues influencing,
  13:41–46
Glaser, W., **4:**43
Goals 2000: The Educate America
 Act, **6:**31, **6:**33

adult literacy/lifelong learning,
6:27–28
advocacy, 6:12–13
applying to child with special
needs, 6:30
mathematics/science, 6:27
overview of, 6:22,
6:23 (tab)–6:24 (tab)
parental participation, 6:29
safe/disciplined and
alcohol-/drug-free
schools, 6:28–29
school completion, 6:24–25
school readiness, 6:22, 6:24
standards, 6:31, 6:33
student achievement/
citizenship, 6:25–26
teacher education/ professional
development, 6:26–27
See also Individuals With
Disabilities Education Act;
No Child Left Behind Act
Goldman, R., 10:26
Good, T., 4:13
Goss v. Lopez, 2:39 (tab)
Grammar, 10:44
Grand mal (tonic-clonic) seizures,
8:23, 8:64
Gray Oral Reading Test–4, 3:37
Greene, J. P., 6:53
Greenwood, C., 3:22, 4:46
Greer, B. B., 8:49
Greer, J. G., 8:49
GRI (Gallaudet Research
Institute), 7:22
Griffin, N. S., 13:11
Grossman, H., 12:24–25
Group data, 3:50
Group homes, 5:30–31, 5:55
Group-administered
tests, 3:27, 3:79
Gruenewald, L., 12:67
Guertin, T. L., 13:45
Guide dogs, 4:55

Hairston v. Drosick, 2:39 (tab)
Hall, V., 4:46
Halo effect errors, 3:62

Haloed, 3:56
Handicapped Children's
Early Education
Assistance Act, 5:11
Handicapped Children's Protection
Act, 2:48–49, 2:55
Harcourt Educational
Measurement, 3:37
Hard-of-hearing
defining, 7:18–19, 7:21, 7:60
See also Hearing impairments
Hart, C. A., 8:30
Haskins, R., 5:15
Havertape, J., 3:20
Head Start, 5:11, 5:15,
5:55, 6:7, 6:9
HeadSmart Schools program,
8:27–28
Hearing acuity, 3:40
Hearing aid, 4:50–51, 4:64, 7:41
troubleshooting, 7:50–51
Hearing impairments
academic characteristics of,
7:23–24
behavioral characteristics of,
7:24–27
central hearing losses, 7:57
cognitive characteristics of,
7:22–23
communication characteristics of,
7:27–28 (tab)
conductive hearing losses,
7:19, 7:56
deaf culture and, 7:26, 7:59
defining, 7:6, 7:18, 7:60
educational implications of,
7:57–58
ethnicity and, 7:26
functional hearing losses, 7:24,
7:25 (tab), 7:60
history of schools for deaf
students, 7:17–18
integrating deaf/hearing
students, 7:26–27
manual communication
for, 7:58
measuring hearing loss, 7:19–21
mixed hearing losses, 7:57

oral communication for, **7**:58
prevalence of, **7**:21–22, **7**:56
senorineural losses, **7**:19, **7**:56–57
signs of, **7**:28 (tab)
teacher tips, **7**:28 (tab)
technology for, **7**:58
total communication for, **7**:58
See also Deaf-and-blind/
    deaf-blind
Heart conditions, **8**:12, **8**:64
Hebbeler, K., **5**:24
Hematomas, **8**:26, **8**:64
subdural, **8**:26, **8**:66
Hemophilia, **8**:13, **8**:59, **8**:64
Henderson, A. T., **5**:42 (tab)
*Hendrick Hudson District Board
    of Education v. Rowley,*
    2:41 (tab), **2**:45–46
Highly qualified teacher, **2**:31–32
Ho, A. S. P., **4**:5
Hobson v. Hansen, **2**:36 (tab)
Hodgkinson, H. L., 44
Holmes, D. L., **8**:29
Home-based programs,
    5:12–14, **5**:55
Homeless child/wards of
    court, **2**:34
Homework buddies, **9**:38–39
Honig v. Doe, **2**:19 (fig), **2**:42 (tab),
    2:49–50
Hospital-based programs, **5**:13–14,
    5:55
Humphries, T., **7**:26
Hunsaker, S. L., **1**:35–36
Hyperactivity-impulsivity, **9**:23–24,
    9:45 (tab), **9**:57
Hyperopia, **7**:9–10, **7**:60

IDEA. *See* Individuals With
    Disabilities Education Act
IDEIA. *See* Individuals With
    Disabilities Education
    Improvement Act
IEP. *See* Individualized education
    programs
IFSP (individualized family service
    plan), **2**:25, **2**:54, **2**:55, **12**:71
Imber-Black, E., **5**:42 (tab)

Immaturity, **3**:47
Immunodeficiency, **8**:12
Inattention, **9**:46–47, **9**:57
Incidental learning, **7**:14
In-class field trip, for math skills,
    12:42 (fig)
Inclusion, **1**:21–22, **1**:41, **6**:21, **6**:38–39
as school reform, **6**:21, **6**:38–39
defining, **6**:45
full, **6**:21
mainstreaming as, **2**:54, **2**:56,
    5:29–30, **5**:56
of student with medical/
    physical/multiple
    disabilities, **8**:56–59,
    8:57 (tab)
of student with mental
    retardation, **12**:67–68
technology role in, **6**:38–39
See also Least restrictive
    environment
Independent living,
    5:23, **5**:30, **5**:32, **8**:31,
    12:31, **12**:55, **12**:58
Independent practice, **4**:40, **10**:36–37
Indirect (consultative)
    services, **1**:26, **1**:40,
    1:41, **5**:12, **5**:55
Individual data, **3**:50
Individual family service plan
    (IFSP), **5**:12, **5**:55, **12**:33
Individualized education programs
    (IEP), **1**:13, **1**:23–24, **2**:54, **8**:43
amendments to, **2**:33
decision-making process
    and, **2**:23–2:24
defining, **1**:42, **2**:55, **3**:79
due process hearing, **2**:21
for student with communication
    disorder, **10**:41–42
for student with mental
    retardation, **12**:6–7,
    12:33, **12**:71
individualized family
    service plan, **2**:25,
    2:54, **2**:55, **12**:71
least restrictive environment
    requirement of, **2**:23

measurable goals requirement of,
2:17, 2:28
prior written notice requirement
of, 2:21
protection in evaluation
procedures provision
of, 2:21
reasons for, 2:17, 2:20
sample of, 2:18 (fig)–19 (fig)
team members required by,
2:20 (fig)
Individualized family service plan
(IFSP), 2:25, 2:54, 2:55, 12:71
Individualized transition plan (ITP),
2:26, 2:55–56, 5:23,
5:56, 12:63, 12:71
Individually administered tests, 3:27
Individuals With Disabilities
Education Act (IDEA),
2:12 (tab), 2:25–26, 2:54
assistive technologies under, 2:26
defining, 2:56
discrimination protection, 1:13
mandates of, 1:12–13,
4:54, 6:37–38
on educational settings, 1:31–32
on emotional disturbance, 11:7–8,
11:35–36
on learning disabilities, 9:7–8, 9:9
on mental retardation, 12:9
on transition services, 5:23
preschool services under,
5:10–11 (fig)
See also Education for All
Handicapped Children Act;
Individuals With Disabilities
Education Act (IDEA),
amendments to; Individuals
With Disabilities Education
Improvement Act; Least
restrictive environment
Individuals With Disabilities
Education Act (IDEA),
amendments to
discipline policies, 2:28–29
individualized education
program, 2:28
manifestation determination, 2:29

parental consent for reevaluation,
2:12 (tab), 2:27
preschoolers, 5:12
streamlined reevaluation, 2:27–28
Individuals With Disabilities
Education Improvement Act
(IDEIA), 2:13, 2:25–26, 2:56
assessment language/
communication mode,
2:32–33
highly qualified teacher
requirement, 2:31–32
homeless child/wards
of court, 2:34
individualized education
program provisions, 2:33
learning disabled
identification, 2:32
special education students in
general education, 2:33
transition planning, 2:33
Inference, 3:61–62, 3:79
Informal interviews, 3:30, 3:79
Informal observations,
3:27, 3:29, 3:44
Informal tests, 3:27, 3:79
Institutions, for adults with
special needs, 5:33
Instruction
computer-assisted, 4:5
defining, 4:5, 4:7, 4:64
teaching as, 4:5
See also Direct instruction,
principles of; Instruction,
adapting for students with
special needs; Instruction,
delivering; Instruction,
evaluating; Instruction,
managing; Instruction,
planning
Instruction, adapting for students
with special
needs, 4:31–38
ability training, 4:39–40
behavior therapy, 4:38
classwide peer tutoring, 4:47
cognitive behavior modification,
4:41, 4:42 (fig)

cognitive skills training, **4:**41, **4:**43
cooperative learning, **4:**45–46
counseling therapy, **4:**43–45
critical thinking, **4:**43
direct instruction, **4:**40
learning strategies training, **4:**45
peer tutoring, **4:**46
peer-directed learning, **4:**46
precision teaching, **4:**39
social skills training, **4:**47–48
Instruction, delivering, **4:**17–23
adjusting instruction, **4:**21 (tab),
    4:22–23
monitoring student learning,
    4:21 (tab)–22
motivating students, **4:**20
overview of, **4:**18 (tab)
presenting content, **4:**17–20
presenting lessons, **4:**17–19
providing relevant
    practice, **4:**20
teaching thinking skills, **4:**19–20
Instruction, evaluating, **4:**23–29
informing students of
    progress, **4:**27
maintaining student progress
    records, **4:**26 (fig)–27
making judgments about student
    performance, **4:**28 (fig)–29
monitoring engaged time, **4:**25
monitoring student
    understanding, **4:**23–25
overview of, **4:**24 (tab)
using data to make decisions,
    4:27–28
Instruction, managing, **4:**14–17
creating positive environment,
    4:16–17
overview of, **4:**15 (tab)
preparing for instruction,
    4:15–16
using time productively, **4:**16
Instruction, planning, **4:**7–14
actively involving
    students, **4:**14
analyzing groupings, **4:**10–11
analyzing task, **4:**10
assessing student skills, **4:**9

communicating realistic
    expectations, **4:**13–14
considering contextual
    variables, **4:**10
deciding how to teach, **4:**11–13
deciding what to teach, **4:**9–11
establishing gaps in actual/
    expected performance, **4:**11
establishing sequence, **4:**10
explicitly stating
    expectations, **4:**14
maintaining high
    standards, **4:**14
monitoring
    performance/replanning
    instruction, **4:**13
overview of, **4:**8 (tab)
pacing, **4:**13
selecting methods/materials,
    4:12–13
setting goals, **4:**12
Instructional adaptations, to
    increase communication/
    motility, **4:**49–50
amplification systems, **4:**51
braille, **4:**52, **7:**10, **7:**13,
    7:15, **7:**16, **7:**34, **7:**35 (tab)
calculators, **4:**53
canes, **4:**55
communication
    boards, **4:**50
computers, **4:**53–54
electronic travel aids, **4:**55–56
guide dogs, **4:**55
hearing aids, **4:**50–51
Kurzweil reading
    machines, **4:**53
optacons, **4:**52–53
prostheses, **4:**56–57
telecommunication devices,
    4:51–52
test modifications, **4:**54
wheelchairs, **4:**56
Instructional diagnosis, **3:**22, **3:**79
Instructional programs, keys
    to success in, **5:**47–50
commitment to normal life
    experiences, **5:**49

commitment to remedial
    programming, 5:49
compatible physical
    environment, 5:49
encouraging appropriate
    behavior, 5:50
individualized planning, 5:48–49
lifelong learning, 5:50
Integration errors, 3:48
Intellectual abilities, 1:34, 1:42, 2:32,
    3:34–37, 9:9
intelligence interviews, 3:36–37
observing intelligence, 3:34, 36
overview of, 3:35 (tab)–36 (tab)
testing intelligence, 3:34
Intellectual functioning, 12:71
Intelligence. See Intellectual abilities
International Baccalaureate
    (IB), 13:26
Interval recording, 3:45, 3:79
Intervention assistance. See
    Prereferral interventions
Intervention assistance team (IAT),
    3:10, 3:79
Interviews, 3:26, 3:30–31
academic achievement,
    assessing, 3:38–39
formal, 3:30
informal, 3:30, 3:79
intelligence, 3:36–37
language, 3:44
perceptual-motor, 3:48
psychological, 3:46–47
structured, 3:30
to assess academic achievement,
    3:38–39
unstructured, 3:30
Irrelevant activity, 11:31, 11:47
Irving Independent School District v.
    Tatro, 2:42 (tab), 2:46, 2:54
ITP (individualized transition plan),
    2:26, 2:55–56, 5:23, 5:56,
    12:63, 12:71

Jackson, D. W., 7:23, 7:24,
    7:27, 7:40, 7:42
Jakob K. Javits Gifted and Talented
    Students Act, 13:11

Jatho, J., 7:26, 7:42
Job coach, 5:25, 5:48, 5:56, 12:54
Johnson, D. W., 4:45
Johnson, F., 12:67
Johnson, N. E., 13:45
Johnson, R. T., 4:45
Jorgensen, J., 12:67
Journals/articles (resources)
    assessment, 3:92–93
    communication disorders,
        10:57–58
    emotional disturbance, 11:60–63
    fundamentals of special
        education, 1:54–55
    gifted and talented child, 13:64
    learning disabilities, 9:67–68
    legal foundations, 2:66
    medical/physical/multiple
        disabilities, 8:80–82
    mental retardation, 12:84–85
    public policy/school
        reform, 6:56
    sensory disabilities, 7:77–79
    transitions, 5:67
Juvenile rheumatoid arthritis,
    8:20, 8:64

Kanner, Leo, 8:29
Kember, D., 4:5
Kentucky School System
    reform, 6:34–35
Kevin T. v. Elmhurst Community
    School District No., 2:44 (tab)
Key Points
    assessment, 3:75–76
    communication disorders,
        10:42–43
    effective instruction, 4:61–62
    emotional disturbance, 11:43–46
    fundamentals, 1:39–40
    gifted and talented child,
        13:51–52
    learning disabilities, 9:55–56
    legal foundations, 2:53–54
    medical/physical/multiple
        disabilities, 8:61–62
    mental retardation,
        12:69–70

public policy/school reform,
  6:43–44
sensory disabilities, **7:**53–58
transitions, **5:**53–54
Key Vocabulary
  assessment, **3:**76–81
  communication disorders,
    10:43–45
  effective instruction, **4:**62–66
  emotional disturbance, **11:**46–47
  families/community agencies,
    5:54–56
  fundamentals, **1:**40–43
  gifted and talented child,
    13:52–53
  learning disabilities, **9:**56–57
  legal foundations, **2:**54–56
  medical/physical/multiple
    disabilities, **8:**62–66
  mental retardation, **12:**70–72
  public policy/school reform,
    6:44–46
  sensory disabilities, **7:**59–62
Kirk, S. A., **9:**51
Klinefelter syndrome, **12:**14, **12:**71
Koestler, F., **7:**8
Koppitz, E. M., **3:**47
Kreimeyer, K. H., **7:**26
Kurzweil reading machines, **4:**53
Kwan, K. P., **4:**5

Lagomarcino, T., **5:**24
Lahey, B. B., **9:**44
Language development, **3:**43–44
  language test components, **3:**43
  using interviews, **3:**44
  using observations, **3:**44
Language disorders, **10:**44
Language evaluation, **10:**44
Larry P v. Riles, **2:**38 (tab)–39 (tab),
  6:10, **6:**45
Larsen, L. M., **13:**11
Larsen, M. D., **13:**11
Latency recording, **3:**46, **3:**80
Law, continuing changes in, **2:**7
Lead poisoning, **8:**11 (tab), **8:**64
Leadership ability, **1:**35, **1:**42,
  13:10, **13:**42

Learning centers,
  for reading, **9:**31
Learning disabilities (LDs)
  academic, **9:**51
  academic characteristics
    of, **9:**23
  assessing, **9:**17–19
  behavioral characteristics of,
    9:23–24
  category growth, **9:**12, **9:**14
  causes of, **9:**15–16
  cognitive characteristics of, **9:**22
  communication characteristics of,
    9:24–25
  criteria for identifying, **9:**8–9
  defining, **9:**7–8, **9:**49–50, **9:**57
  defining, variations by state,
    9:51–52
  developmental, **9:**51
  discrepancy criterion
    removal, **9:**9
  distribution of students
    with, by state, **9:**13
    (tab)–**9:**14 (tab)
  growth in specific learning
    disabilities category, **9:**11–12
  physical characteristics
    of, **9:**23
  prevalence of, **9:**11
  subtypes of, **9:**51
  transition of students
    with, **9:**52
  See also Learning disabilities
    (LDs), improving classroom
    behavior for students with;
    Learning disabilities (LDs),
    teaching students with
Learning disabilities (LDs),
  improving classroom behavior
  for students with
  daily reports, **9:**37 (fig)
  homework buddies,
    9:38–39
  study skills, **9:**37–39
  work habits, **9:**35–37
Learning disabilities (LDs),
  teaching students with,
  9:25–41

general interventions, **9:**26 (tab)
math skills, **9:**32–33
reading skills, **9:**27–32
social relations, **9:**39–41
study skills, **9:**37–39
trends/issues influencing
   teaching of, **9:**49–52
work habits, **9:**35–37
written language skills, **9:**33–35
Learning strategies training,
   4:45, **4:**64
Least restrictive environment (LRE),
   1:13, **1:**27–28, **2:**23, **2:**41, **2:**54,
   2:56, **12:**61
   defining, **5:**30, **5:**56, **12:**71
Ledesma, J., **4:**5
Lee, V. E., **5:**15
Leff, D., **7:**11, **7:**15
Legal fees, **2:**42 (tab), **2:**46–48
Legal foundations, of special
   education
   balance perspective in, **2:**51–52
   brief history of, **2:**9–10
   early issues in, **2:**44–45
   overview of important laws,
      2:10–11
   overview of influential court
      cases, **2:**36 (tab)–44 (tab)
   Supreme Court rulings, **2:**45–50
   See also *individual laws and
      individual cases*
Legally blind, **7:**9, **7:**60
Legg-Calvé-Perthes disease,
   8:21, **8:**64
Lehr, C., **5:**18
Lehr, F., **9:**28
Lemon v. Bossier Parish School Board,
   2:38 (tab)
Leukemia, **8:**11 (tab), **8:**64
Leventhal, J. D., **7:**36
Levine, D. U., **4:**5–6
Levy, S. E., **8:**15
Lewis, R. B., **8:**56–58, **8:**57 (tab),
   10:18–20
Lieberman, L., **7:**29
Lifelong learning, **5:**50, **6:**27–28
Light v. Parkway School District,
   2:43 (tab)

Liles, C., **8:**15–16, **8:**43, **8:**55–56
Limb deficiencies, **8:**21–22, **8:**64
Listening-skills training,
   7:34, **7:**35 (tab)
Living arrangements, for adults
   with special needs
   alternative living unit, **5:**31
   foster homes, **5:**31–32
   group homes, **5:**30–31
   independent living, **5:**32
   institutions, **5:**33
Lloyd, J., **4:**40
Logical errors, **3:**62
Long, E., **12:**67
*Lora v. New York City Board of
   Education,* **2:**40 (tab)–41 (tab)
Loudness, **7:**19–20, **7:**60
Louisiana Department of Education,
   13:12
Low vision, **7:**60–61
Luckner, J., **7:**24, **7:**38, **7:**42, **7:**50
Luetke-Stahlman, B., **7:**24, **7:**42, **7:**50
Lynch, E. W., **8:**56–58, **8:**57 (tab)

Mainstreaming, **2:**54, **2:**56,
   5:29–30, **5:**56
   See also *Least restrictive
      environment*
Mangrum, C. II, **5:**26
Manifestation determination,
   2:29, **2:**56
Manual movements, **7:**40, **7:**61
Marburger, C. L., **5:**42 (tab)
Marder, C., **5:**24
Marland, S., **13:**41–42
Maryland State Department of
   Education, **13:**11
Mastery, defining, **9:**32
Mathematics, improving,
   6:27, **9:**32–33, **9:**34 (fig)
McBurnett, K., **9:**44
McKinney, J. D., **9:**51
McMeniman, M. M., **4:**5
Measures of process disorders,
   9:18–19
Medical disabilities, **8:**9–16
   AIDS, **8:**12–13
   cystic fibrosis, **8:**12

fetal alcohol syndrome, **8**:14
heart conditions, **8**:12
hemophilia, **8**:13–14
identification by medical
    symptoms, **8**:9–10
maternal cocaine use, **8**:14–15
medically fragile/technology
    dependent groups, **8**:15–16
other health impairments,
    8:10–11 (tab)
prevalence of, **8**:10
special health problems, **8**:14–15
Medical procedures, to ensure
    appropriate education,
    2:46, **2**:48, **2**:54
Medical treatment, for emotional
    disturbance, **11**:37–38
Medically fragile, **8**:15, **8**:64
Medical/physical/multiple
    disabilities
academic characteristics
    of, **8**:38
behavioral characteristics of,
    8:39–40
cognitive characteristics of,
    8:37–38
communication characteristics of,
    8:40–41
distribution of child with, **8**:7–8
    (fig)
home *vs.* institutional care for,
    8:55–56
inclusion of student with, **8**:56
inclusion of student with,
    overcoming barriers to,
    8:56–59, **8**:57 (tab)
medical disabilities, **8**:9–16,
    8:10–11 (tab)
multiple disabilities, **8**:33–35
physical characteristics of, **8**:39
physical disabilities,
    8:17–31, **8**:25 (tab)
relationship to federal disability
    categories, **8**:7 (fig)
See also Medical/
    physical/multiple
    disabilities, teaching
    students with

Medical/physical/multiple
    disabilities, teaching students
    with, **8**:43–53
adapting instruction, **8**:47–49
common adaptations, **8**:49–50
encouraging socialization, **8**:53
facilitating communication,
    8:50–52
fostering independence, **8**:52–53
general tips for, **8**:45 (tab)
identifying disabilities, **8**:44
key areas of assistance, **8**:46–47
questions to ask about, **8**:44, **8**:45
    (tab)–**8**:46 (tab)
residual functioning, **8**:52–53
Mental retardation, **1**:16, **1**:42
academic characteristics of, **12**:30
as primary/secondary condition,
    12:28
behavioral characteristics
    of, **12**:31
characteristics of, **12**:2 (tab)
cognitive characteristics
    of, **12**:30
communication characteristics of,
    12:31–32
defining, **12**:6, **12**:9, **12**:71
genetic conditions as cause
    of, **12**:13–14
graduation rates of student with,
    12:63–64
health problems as cause
    of, **12**:15
inclusion of student with,
    12:67–68
individualized education
    program, **12**:6–7
learning environments for
    student with, **12**:67
mild/moderate/severe/
    profound retardation, **12**:10
    (fig)–**12**:11 (tab)
physical characteristics of,
    12:30–31
prevalence of, **12**:11
preventing, **12**:62 (tab)
problems during pregnancy/
    birth as cause of, **12**:15

recent advances in treatment/
    services, **12**:65–67
self-determination
    and, **12**:64
transitioning from school to
    work, **12**:63–64
See also Mental retardation,
    diagnosing; Mental
    retardation, teaching
    students with
Mental retardation, diagnosing,
    12:17–25
adaptive behavior area,
    12:17, **12**:19–25
adaptive behavior, defining,
    12:21
adaptive behavior scales, **12**:21
adaptive skill areas evaluated,
    12:21 (tab)–23 (tab)
age-related criteria for, **12**:24–25
intellectual functioning
    area, **12**:17
Mental retardation, teaching
    students with, **12**:33–51
by making adaptations, **12**:33–34
family tips for, **12**:34,
    12:36 (tab)
functional math skills,
    12:41–42 (fig)
functional reading skills, **12**:38–41
    (fig), **12**:39 (fig), **12**:40
    (fig), **12**:41 (fig), 40 (fig)
functional writing, **12**:40
general interventions for,
    12:37 (tab)
grading systems for, **12**:47–49
individualized education
    program, **12**:33
individualized family services
    plan, **12**:33
leisure skills, **12**:50–51
school adaptive behavior,
    12:45–49
task analysis, **12**:43–45
task completion, **12**:38
teacher tips for, **12**:35 (tab)
trends/issues influencing,
    12:61–64

work skills, **12**:49–50
    See also Severe disabilities,
        teaching student with
Metropolitan Achievement Tests, **3**:37
Meyer, C., **3**:39
Meyer, L. H., **12**:55
Michaud, L. J., **8**:25, **8**:26, **8**:27
Mild/moderate/severe/
    profound retardation,
    12:10 (fig)–**12**:11 (tab)
Miller, L., **3**:21
Minitests, **9**:30 (fig), **9**:57
*Minnesota Standards for
    Services to Gifted and
    Talented Students,* **13**:12
Minnesota State Advisory
    Council for the Gifted
    and Talented, **13**:12
Mizuko, M., **10**:16
Mobility, **7**:14, **7**:61
Mobility aids, **7**:34, **7**:35 (tab)
Mock, D., **9**:17
Molloy, D. E., **9**:17–18
Moore, S. D., **1**:35–36
Moores, D., **7**:17, **7**:21,
    7:23, **7**:24–25, **7**:26, **7**:42
Moran, M., **6**:41
Morgan, P. L., **9**:17
Morphology, **10**:10–11, **10**:44
Mowat Sensor, **4**:55–56
Muir, S., **7**:38
Multiple disabilities, **8**:34–35
Multiple intelligences, **13**:43, **13**:53
Multiple or severe
    disabilities, **1**:16, **1**:42
    See also Severe disabilities,
        teaching student with
Multiple sclerosis, **8**:20–21
Murphy, D. S., **8**:56–58, **8**:57 (tab)
Muscular dystrophy, **8**:19–20, **8**:65
Myelomeningocele, **8**:24
Myopia, **7**:9, **7**:61

NAGC (National Association for
    Gifted Children), **13**:25–27
Nania, P. A., **5**:18
*A Nation at Risk: The Imperative for
    Educational Reform,* **6**:19–20

National Association for
 Gifted Children (NAGC),
 13:25–27
National Association
 of the Deaf, **7:**42
National Autistic Society, **8:**28
National Center for Education
 Statistics, **1:**31, **5:**9, **5:**10
National Commission on Excellence
 in Education, **6:**19–20
National Council on Educational
 Standards and Testing, **6:**31–32
National Dissemination Center for
 Children with Disabilities
 (NICHY), **11:**44–46
National Education Goals,
 5:10, **6:**19–20, **6:**45
National Educational
 Standards and Improvement
 Council, **6:**31
National Governors' Association,
 6:20, **6:**34
National Head Injury Foundation
 (NHIF), **8:**27–28
National Information Center, **10:**38
National Institute on Deafness and
 Other Communication
 Disorders Information
 Clearinghouse, **7:**58
National Joint Committee on
 Learning Disabilities (NJCLD),
 9:15, **9:**50
National Research Council, **1:**13
Nechita, A., **1:**35
Needs assessments, **4:**41, **4:**64
Nephrosis/nephritis,
 8:11 (tab), **8:**65
Neurological disorders, **8:**22–25
 cerebral palsy, **8:**23–24
 epilepsy, **8:**23
 overview of, **8:**25 (tab)
 spina bifida, **8:**24
 spinal cord injury, **8:**24–25
Newland, T. E.,
 7:12–13, **7:**30
Newman, L., **5:**24
NHIF (National Head Injury
 Foundation), **8:**27–28

NICHY (National Dissemination
 Center for Children with
 Disabilities), **11:**44–46
NJCLD (National Joint Committee
 on Learning Disabilities),
 9:15, **9:**50
No Child Left Behind Act, **2:**12 (tab),
 2:29–31, **2:**54, **6:**10, **6:**37–38, **6:**45
Nonattention (distractibility),
 11:29–30, **11:**47
Noncategorical, **12:**18, **12:**71
Noncompliance (oppositional
 behavior), **11:**22–24, **11:**47
Nonmanual movements, **7:**40, **7:**61
Nonphysical disruptions,
 11:27–28, **11:**47
Normal field of vision, **7:**9, **7:**61
Normalization, **12:**61, **12:**72
Normative peer comparisons,
 4:28, **4:**64
Norm-referenced tests,
 3:29, **3:**80, **4:**9, **4:**64
Norms, **3:**8–9, **3:**80
Nystagmus, **7:**10, **7:**61

Objective-referenced test. *See*
 Criterion-referenced tests
Observations, **3:**25–26, **3:**29–30
 active, **3:**29, **3:**77
 defining, **3:**80
 formal, **3:**29
 informal, **3:**27, **3:**29, **3:**44
 language, **3:**44
 of achievement, **3:**38
 of sensory acuity, **3:**40–41
 passive, **3:**29, **3:**80
 perceptual-motor, **3:**48
Occupational and
 social skills, **3:**42
OCR (Optical character recognition),
 7:36 (tab),
 7:38, **7:**61
Ocular motility, **7:**10, **7:**61
Oden, M., **13:**20, **13:**41, **13:**42
Office of Civil Rights, **6:**11, **6:**13
Office of Educational Research
 and Improvement, **13:**45,
 13:48, **13:**49

Office of Special
    Education Programs (OSEP),
    6:13–14, **6:**45
Ogbu, J. U., **13:**48
On Your Own
    assessment, **3:**89
    communication
        disorders, **10:**55
    effective instruction, **4:**73
    emotional disturbance, **11:**55–56
    families/community
        agencies, **5:**63
    fundamentals of special
        education, **1:**51
    gifted and talented child,
        13:61–62
    learning disabilities, **9:**65–66
    legal foundations of special
        education, **2:**63
    medical/physical/multiple
        disabilities, **8:**73–74
    mental retardation, **12:**79
    public policy/school
        reform, **6:**53
    sensory disabilities, **7:**69–71
Ooms, T., **5:**42 (tab)
Operant conditioning,
    4:38, **4:**65
Opportunity-to-learn (OTL)
    standards, **4:**46, **6:**12,
    6:33, **6:**45
Oppositional behavior
    (noncompliance),
    11:22–24, **11:**47
Optacons, **4:**52–53
Optical character recognition (OCR),
    7:36 (tab), **7:**38, **7:**61
Oral communication,
    for students with
    vision/hearing impairments,
    7:39–40, **7:**39 (tab)
Organizations (resources)
    assessment, **3:**93
    communication disorders,
        10:58–59
    effective instruction, **4:**77
    emotional disturbance,
        11:63–65

fundamentals of special
    education, **1:**54–55
gifted and talented child, **13:**65
learning disabilities, **9:**68–69
medical/physical/multiple
    disabilities, **8:**83–84
mental retardation, **12:**86–87
public policy/school reform,
    6:56–57
sensory disabilities, **7:**79–85
transitions, **5:**68
Orientation, **7:**14, **7:**61
Ornstein, A. C., **4:**5–6
Orr, A. L., **7:**7, **7:**11, **7:**13,
    7:14, **7:**15, **7:**34
Orr, S., **4:**5
Orthopedic impairments,
    8:17–18, **8:**65
    prevalence of, **8:**18
Orthopedic or other health
    impairments, **1:**16–17, **1:**42
Orthosis, **8:**52, **8:**65
Osborn, J., **9:**28
OSEP (Office of Special Education
    Programs), **6:**13–14, **6:**45
Osteogenesis imperfecta, **8:**20, **8:**65
Osteomyelitis, **8:**21, **8:**65
O'Sullivan, P. J., **5:**18
OTL (Opportunity-to-learn)
    standards, **4:**46, **6:**12, **6:**33, **6:**45
Outcomes-based
    accountability, **3:**23, **6:**35

Pace, **4:**13, **4:**65
Panitch v. State of Wisconsin,
    2:40 (tab)
Parental participation, **6:**29
Partially sighted, **7:**61
PASE v. Hannon, **2:**41 (tab)
Passive observation, **3:**29
Pathsounder, **4:**55
Paul, P. V., **7:**23, **7:**24,
    7:27, **7:**40, **7:**42
Paulson, F., **3:**39
Paulson, P., **3:**39
Peavey, K. O., **7:**11, **7:**15
Peck, C. A., **12:**55
Peer tutoring, **4:**46–47, **4:**65

Peer tutoring, classwide,
    4:47, 4:63
Peer-directed learning, **4:46**
Pennsylvania Association of Retarded
    Citizens v. Commonwealth of
    Pennsylvania, **12:**65–66
PEP (protection in evaluation
    procedures), **1:**13, **1:**42,
    2:21–23, **2:**56
Perceptual-motor development,
    3:47–48
Perceptual-motor interviews, **3:**48
Perceptual-motor observations, **3:**48
Perceptual-motor tests, **3:**47–48, **3:**80
Performance assessment,
    3:24, **3:**80
Perret, Y. M., **8:**22, **8:**47
Perseveration errors, **3:**38, **3:**48
Perspective
    assessment, **3:**73–74
    communication disorders,
        10:35–38
    effective instruction, **4:**59–60
    emotional disturbance, **11:**39–41
    fundamentals, **1:**37–38
    gifted and talented, **13:**47–49
    learning disabilities, **9:**53–54
    legal foundations, **2:**51–52
    medical/physical/multiple
        disabilities, **8:**55–59
    mental retardation, **12:**65–68
    public policy/school reform,
        6:37–42
    sensory disabilities, **7:**47–51
    transitions, **5:**51–52
Petit mal seizures, **8:**23, **8:**65
Pfiffner, L. J., **9:**44
Phenylketonuria (PKU),
    12:14, **12:**72
Phonetic cues, **9:**29, **9:**57
Phonology, **10:**10–11, **10:**44
Physical disabilities, **8:**17–31
    autism, **8:**28–31
    craniofacial anomalies, **8:**22
    defining, **8:**65
    juvenile rheumatoid
        arthritis, **8:**20
    Legg-Calvé-Perthes disease, **8:**21

limb deficiencies, **8:**21–22
    multiple sclerosis, **8:**20–21
    muscular dystrophy, **8:**19–20
    neurological disorders, **8:**22–25
    orthopedic impairments, **8:**17–18
    osteogenesis imperfecta, **8:**20
    poliomyelitis, **8:**18–19
    traumatic brain injury, **1:**17, **1:**43,
        8:25–28, **8:**66
Physical disruptions, **11:**27, **11:**47
Pilmer, S. L., **8:**15
Pogrund, R. L., **7:**7, **7:**11
Poliomyelitis, **8:**18–19, **8:**65
Portfolios, **3:**26, **3:**39, **3:**80
Post-school interventions, **5:**50, **5:**56
Post-school transitions,
    5:23, **5:**24–25, **5:**37
Poteet, J., **3:**21
Powers, M. D., **8:**29, **8:**30
Pragmatics, **10:**11, **10:**44
Pratt, S., **8:**30
Precision teaching, **4:**39, **4:**65
Prereferral interventions
    defining, **1:**9, **1:**22, **1:**42, **3:**80
    determining eligibility, **1:**22
    evolution of, **1:**11–12
    growth in population receiving,
        1:19–20
    individualized education
        programs
        (See Individualized
            education programs)
    perspective on, **1:**37–38
    process evaluation, **1:**24
    purpose of, **3:**11
Preschool
    attendance increase, **5:**9–10
    early intervention during, **5:**9–10
    Individuals With Disabilities
        Education Act and, **5:**10–12,
        5:11 (fig)
    transition to K-12 education
        system, **5:**18–19
    Ypsilanti Perry Preschool Project,
        5:15–16
President's Commission on
    Excellence in Special
    Education, **1:**13

Private school, **2:**42 (tab),
   2:46–47, **2:**54
Process disorders, **9:**19, **9:**57
Program evaluation
   defining, **3:**80
   large-scale, **3:**16–17
   teacher's own, **3:**17
Programmed learning,
   13:37, **13:**39, **13:**53
Progress evaluation, **1:**24, **3:**80
Prostheses/prosthetic devices,
   4:56–57, **4:**65, **8:**65
Protection in evaluation procedures
   (PEP), **1:**13, **1:**42, **2:**21–23, **2:**56
Psychoeducational
   assessment, **3:**9, **3:**81
Psychological development,
   assessing, **3:**45–47
   personality tests, **3:**45
   psychological interviews, **3:**46–47
   psychological observations,
      3:45–46
Psychological interviews, **3:**46–47
Public Law 94–142. *See*
   Education for All
   Handicapped Children Act
Public policy
   impact on special education,
      6:39–40
   political effects on, **6:**10–11
   See also School reform
Pupil unit allocation method,
   6:16–17
Purcell, J. H., **13:**45

Quay, H., **3:**46

Rakes, T., **3:**21
Randomization without
   replacement, **4:**60
RAP mnemonic, **4:**45
Rapport, establishing, 60
Reading, improving
   analytical programs for,
      9:27, **9:**56
   fostering motivation/interest,
      9:30–32
   reading comprehension, **9:**28–30

sight word recognition, **9:**28
   taped texts for, **9:**6
   whole language programs for,
      9:27, **9:**57
Reading Excellence Act, **6:**20
Reading First, **2:**30–31, **6:**10, **6:**20
Reality therapy, **4:**43, **4:**65
Reber, M., **8:**30
Receptive language, **10:**44
Redl, F., **4:**44
Referral, **1:**22, **1:**42
   See also Prereferral interventions
Reflection
   assessment, **3:**3–4, **3:**85–87
   communication disorders,
      10:5, **10:**51
   effective instruction, **4:**4, **4:**70
   emotional disturbance, **11:**3–4,
      11:51–52
   families/community agencies,
      5:3–4, **5:**59–60
   fundamentals of special
      education, **1:**4, **1:**48
   gifted and talented
      child, **13:**3–4, **13:**57–58
   learning disabilities,
      9:3–4, **9:**62
   legal foundations of special
      education, **2:**4, **2:**60
   medical/physical/multiple
      disabilities, **8:**3, **8:**69–70
   mental retardation, **12:**3–4,
      12:75–76
   public policy/school
      reform, **6:**3, **6:**49
   sensory disabilities, **7:**3, **7:**65
Regular education initiative (REI),
   6:21, **6:**45
Rehabilitation Act, **2:**53, **9:**44
Reichert, E. S., **13:**45
Reis, S. M., **13:**45
Related services, **1:**26, **5:**12, **10:**42
   as part of individualized
      education program,
      1:23, **11:**45, **12:**33
   defining, **1:**42–43, **6:**45
   growth in numbers receiving,
      1:19–20

mandated, **1:**31, **2:**48, **6:**40, **8:**17,
    8:43, **12:**9
Related services personnel,
    1:20, **3:**12
Reliability, **3:**50, **3:**81
Reliability coefficient,
    3:50, **3:**81
Remedial education, **3:**10, **3:**81
Renzulli, J., **13:**18, **13:**43
Representativeness, **3:**50–51, **3:**81
Residual functioning,
    8:52–53, **8:**65
Resources
    assessment, **3:**91–93
    communication disorders,
        10:57–59
    effective instruction, **4:**75–77
    emotional disturbance, **11:**57–65
    families/community agencies,
        5:65–68
    fundamentals of special
        education, **1:**53–55
    gifted and talented child,
        13:63–65
    learning disabilities, **9:**67
    legal foundations of special
        education, **2:**65–66
    medical/physical/multiple
        disabilities, **8:**75–83
    mental retardation, **12:**81–87
    public policy/school reform,
        6:55–57
    sensory disabilities, **7:**73–85
Respondent conditioning,
    4:38, **4:**65
Response to intervention (RTI),
    9:17, **9:**18
Rheumatic fever,
    8:11 (tab), **8:**65
Rogers, C., **4:**44
Rogers, M., **4:**49
Rogers, P. A., **7:**7, **7:**11,
    7:13, **7:**14, **7:**15, **7:**34
Rose, L. C., **11:**39
Rotation errors, **3:**48
RTI (response to intervention),
    9:17, **9:**18
Rubrics, **3:**31

Rusch, F., **5:**24
Ryser, G., **7:**15

Saccuzzo, D. P., **13:**45
Safe schools, **6:**28–29
Samuelowicz, K., **4:**5
Schaller, J., **7:**15
Schattman, R., **12:**59
Schnur, E., **5:**15
School reform, **6:**19–35
    Goals 2000 (*See* Goals 2000: The
        Educate America Act)
    impact on special
        education, **6:**35
    inclusion as, **6:**21, **6:**38–39
    national goals, **6:**19–20
    national standards, **6:**30–33
    opportunity-to-learn standards,
        4:46, **6:**12, **6:**33, **6:**45
    regular education
        initiative/inclusion, **6:**21
    school restructuring,
        6:33–34, **6:**45
    See also Public policy
School restructuring,
    6:33–34, **6:**45
School-based enterprises, **5:**46, **5:**56
Schoolhouse giftedness, **13:**43, **13:**53
Schrier, E. M., **7:**36
Schumaker, J., **4:**45
Schweinhart, L., **5:**16
Screening, **3:**7–8
    defining, **3:**81
    early, **3:**8–9
    late, **3:**9–10
    tests for, **3:**28
    See also Protection in evaluation
        procedures
Section 504 of the Rehabilitation
    Act, **2:**11 (tab), **2:**13,
    2:14–15, **2:**56, **4:**54
Seizures
    grand mal (tonic-clonic),
        8:23, **8:**64
    petit mal, **8:**23, **8:**65
Self-Assessment/Answer Key
    assessment, **3:**1–3,
        3:83–85, **3:**87

communication disorders, **10:**1–5,
10:47–51, **10:**53–54
effective instruction, **4:**1–3,
4:67–69, **4:**71
emotional disturbance, **11:**1–3,
11:49–51, **11:**53
families/community agencies,
5:1–3, **5:**57–59, **5:**61
fundamentals of
special education,
1:1–4, **1:**45–47, **1:**49
gifted and talented child, **13:**1–3,
13:55–57, **13:**59
learning disabilities, **9:**1–3,
9:59–61, **9:**63
legal foundations of
special education,
2:1, **2:**57–60, **2:**61
medical/physical/multiple
disabilities, **8:**1–3,
8:67–69, **8:**71
mental retardation, **12:**1–3,
12:73–75, **12:**77
public policy/school reform,
6:1, **6:**47–49, **6:**51
sensory disabilities, **7:**1–3,
7:63–65, **7:**67
Self-care, **12:**47, **12:**57
Self-contained class, **4:**28, **4:**65
Self-determination, **12:**64, **12:**72
Self-direction, **12:**46–47
Self-help skills, **3:**42
Semantics, **10:**11, **10:**44
Sensitivity errors, **3:**62
Sensorineural hearing loss, **7:**19, **7:**61
Sensory acuity, assessing,
3:39–**3:**41 (fig)
Sensory disabilities, teaching
student with
assistive listening, **7:**41
collaboration role in, **7:**52
communication system, **7:**41–42
cued speech, **7:**40–41
eliminating barriers overview,
7:34–38, **7:**35 (tab)–36 (tab),
7:39 (tab)
empowering student, **7:**47–48
fostering independence, **7:**42–45

future of, **7:**52
improving communication
overview, **7:**39 (tab)
oral communication, **7:**39–40
positive interaction tips, **7:**44–45
sign systems, **7:**40
supporting accommodations for,
7:49–51
technology to eliminate barriers,
7:34, **7:**36–38
telecommunication devices, **7:**41
total communication, **7:**40
understanding characteristics
specific to, **7:**49
See also Deaf-and-blind/
deaf-blind; Hearing
impairments; Visual
impairments
Sentner, S. M., **4:**5
Severe disabilities, teaching student
with, **12:**53–59
communication considerations,
12:56–57
community living and, **12:**57–58
curriculum considerations, **12:**56
defining severe disabilities,
12:54–55
instructional approaches,
12:58–59
mobility, **12:**57
prevalence of, **12:**55
self-care and, **12:**57
Shape distortions, **3:**48
Sheltered/supported employment,
5:25, **5:**56
Shin, H., **6:**33
Siblings, effect of exceptionalities
on, **5:**36–37
Sickle-cell anemia, **8:**11 (tab), **8:**66
Sigafoos, J., **7:**26
Sign language, **7:**39 (tab), **7:**40
Silverman, L. K., **13:**44
Singleton, P., **7:**47
Site-based management,
6:34, **6:**35, **6:**46
Six-hour retarded child, 41
Skilled examiner, **3:**59–61
Skinner, D., **4:**5

Skull fractures, **8:**26, **8:**66
Smith, J., 14–15
Smith v. Robinson, **2:**42 (tab), **2:**47–49
Snellen Wall Chart, **3:**40
Social interactions, improving
    for student with emotional
        disturbance, **11:**13–14
    for student with learning
        disabilities, **9:**39–41
Social problems, **11:**17, **11:**47
Social skills, **7:**15
    occupational skills and, **3:**42
    school adaptive behavior and,
        12:45–46
    training in, **4:**47–48, **4:**65, **12:**45–46
Social values, affect on special
        education, **6:**8–10
Software
    math, **12:**41
    sight word recognition, **9:**28
Sonicguide, **4:**56
Spastic cerebral palsy, **8:**23–24
Special education
    categories of, **1:**15–17
    current reforms in, **6:**40
        (*See also* Public policy;
        School reform)
    defining, **1:**43
    future of, **6:**41
    social values and, **6:**8–10
    See also Special education,
        economic factors driving
Special education, economic factors
        driving, **6:**13–17
    allocation methods, **6:**16–17
    federal review of state
        plans, **6:**14
    funding competition, **6:**15
    OSEP programs, **6:**13–14
    research priorities, **6:**15
Special education process. *See*
    Prereferral interventions
Special educators, continuing
        demand for, **1:**20
Specific learning disabilities
    defining, **1:**17, **1:**43
    See also Learning disabilities
Spectrum disorder, **8:**29

Speece, D., **9:**17–18
Speech disorders, **10:**44
    articulation disorder, **10:**9–10
    fluency disorder, **10:**10
    voice disorder, **10:**10
Speech evaluation, **10:**44
Speech or language impairments,
        1:17, **1:**43
Speech-language pathologist,
        10:17–18, **10:**39–41, **10:**44
Spina bifida, **8:**24, **8:**66
Spinal cord injuries, **8:**24–25, **8:**66
Spooner, F., **12:**43
Stahl, S. A., **9:**28
Standard behavior chart, **4:**39, **4:**65
Standards
    defining, **6:**31, **6:**46
    legislation on, **6:**37–38
    national, **6:**30–33
    opportunity-to-learn, **4:**46, **6:**12,
        6:33, **6:**45
Stark, J., **10:**27
Stem, B., **12:**43
Stereotypes, **3:**56, **3:**81
Stern, B., **12:**43
Stern, J., **6:**13
Sternberg, R. J., **13:**43
Strabismus, **7:**10, **7:**61
Strichart, S. S., **5:**26
Structured interview, **3:**30
Stuart, M., **7:**29
Student progress records,
        4:26 (fig)–27
Stuttering. *See* Fluency disorder
Subdural hematomas, **8:**26, **8:**66
Summative evaluation, **4:**23, **4:**65
Supported employment,
        5:25, **5:**56
Swan, M., **13:**33
Syntax, **10:**10–11
Synthetic speech devices,
        7:37, **7:**62

TA (transactional analysis),
        4:44, **4:**65
Talented, defining, **13:**53
TASH (The Association for Persons
        with Severe Handicaps), **12:**55

Task analysis, **3**:22, **3**:81, **4**:10, **4**:40,
   4:65, **12**:43–45, **12**:72
Task avoidance, **11**:31–33, **11**:47
Task Force on DSM-IV, **9**:45 (tab)
Taylor, R. L., **3**:7
Teacher
   egalitarian, **4**:59–60
   highly qualified, **2**:31–32
   humanitarian, **4**:60
   radomizer, **4**:60
Teacher education/professional
   development, **6**:26–27
Teacher training, reform in, **6**:40
Teacher unit allocation
   method, **6**:16
Teaching
   defining, **4**:5, **4**:7, **4**:66
   precision, **4**:39
   principles for effective, **4**:5–6
   tips for, **6**:42
Technical career programs, **5**:45–46
Technology, to increase
   communication/motility,
   4:53–54
Technology dependent, **8**:15–16, **8**:66
Tech-prep programs,
   5:45–46, **5**:56
Telecommunication
   devices, **4**:51–52, **4**:66,
   7:39 (tab), **7**:41, **7**:42
Temper tantrums, **11**:47
Terman, L., **13**:20, **13**:41, **13**:42
Test, D. W., **12**:43
Test modifications, **4**:54
Testing/tests
   achievement, **3**:37, **3**:77
   criterion-referenced, **3**:28–29,
      3:77–78, **4**:9, **4**:64
   defining, **3**:25, **3**:81
   diagnostic, **3**:28, **3**:78
   formal, **3**:27, **3**:79
   group-administered, **3**:27, **3**:79
   group/individual tests, **3**:27
   informal measures, **3**:27
   norm-/criterion-referenced tests,
      3:28–29
   norm-referenced, **3**:29,
      3:80, **4**:9, **4**:64

screening/diagnostics, **3**:28
test content, **3**:29
test development, **3**:52–54
test fairness, **3**:55–56
test formats, **3**:27–28
test modifications, **4**:54
The Association for Persons
   with Severe Handicaps
   (TASH), **12**:55
Thematic units, **9**:57
Thinking skills, **4**:19–20
Thomas, D., **5**:15
Thurlow, M. L., **3**:71,
   5:18, **6**:9, **6**:33
Thurlow, M. L., Wiley, H. I.,
   & Bielinski, J., **6**:60
Time sampling recording,
   3:46, **3**:81
Timothy W. v. Rochester,
   New Hampshire,
   School District, **2**:5–6,
   2:42 (tab)–43 (tab)
Tinker v. Des Moines Independent
   Community School District,
   2:36 (tab)–37 (tab)
Tonic-clonic (grand mal) seizures,
   8:23, **8**:64
Total communication, for student
   with vision/hearing
   impairments, **7**:39 (tab), **7**:40
Transactional analysis
   (TA), **4**:44, **4**:65
Transition plans, **5**:17–18
   individualized, **2**:26, **2**:55–56,
      5:23, **5**:56, **12**:63, **12**:71
Transition services, **2**:26, **2**:33,
   2:56, **5**:6
   defining, **5**:23, **5**:56
   See also Community
      collaboration
Transitions
   effect on families, **5**:36–37
   See also Transition plans;
      Transition services;
      Transitions, types of
Transitions, types of, **5**:17–23
   continued education, **5**:26–27
   dropping out, **5**:20–23, **5**:21 (tab)

during school, **5:**19
employment/financial
  independence, **5:**24–25
everyday, **5:**19
post-school, **5:**23,
  5:24–25, **5:**37
preschool to K-12 education
  system, **5:**18–19
within general education
  classrooms, **5:**20
Traumatic brain injury (TBI), **1:**17,
  1:43, **8:**17, **8:**25–28, **8:**66
Tuberculosis, **8:**11 (tab), **8:**66
20/20 vision, **7:**8

Udvari-Solner, A., **12:**67
Unified system, **6:**35, **6:**46
Unstructured interview, **3:**30
U.S. Congress, **2:**16
U.S. Department of Education, **1:**11,
  1:15, **1:**19–20, **7:**10, **7:**11, **7:**21,
  7:30, **7:**56–58, **8:**6, **8:**29, **8:**34,
  9:14 (tab), **12:**11, **12:**61
U.S. Office of Civil Rights, **6:**46
Uslan, M. M., **7:**36

Validity, **3:**51–54, **3:**81
VanDeventer, P., **12:**67
Visual acuity, **3:**40, **7:**8, **7:**62
Visual functioning, **7:**10
Visual impairments, **1:**16, **1:**40
  academic/cognitive
    characteristics of,
    7:11–14, **7:**54–55
  appropriate literacy medium,
    7:16
  behavioral characteristics of,
    7:14–15
  brief history of special education
    and, **7:**7
  communication characteristics of,
    7:15–16
  defining, **7:**6, **7:**8, **7:**9, **7:**62
  eligibility for students with,
    7:9–10, **7:**55
  environmental modifications
    for, **7:**13
  focusing difficulties, **7:**9–10

physical characteristics of, **7:**14
  prevalence of, **7:**10–11, **7:**54
  signs of, **7:**12 (tab)
  teaching modifications for,
    7:13–14
  teaching tips, **7:**16 (tab)
  technological aid for, **7:**13
  visual functioning, **7:**10
Vocabulary, defining, **10:**45
Voice disorder, **10:**10, **10:**45

Wagner, M., **5:**22, **5:**24
Walker, H. M., **3:**46
Walker, R., **6:**34
Wang, M. C., **4:**31–32
Ward, M., **4:**53
Wards of court/homeless
  child, **2:**34
Warner, M., **4:**45
Washington v. Davis, **2:**39 (tab)
Watson v. City of Cambridge, Mass.,
  2:36 (tab)
Web sites (resources)
  effective instruction, **4:**75
  sensory disabilities, **7:**73
Weber, J., **11:**36
Wehman, P., **5:**44–45
Weikart, D., **5:**16
Weiss, J. A., **5:**18
Wheelchairs, **4:**56
Whole language program,
  9:27, **9:**57
Whorton, D., **4:**46
Wiederholt, L., **3:**37
Withdrawal, **3:**47, **11:**6, **11:**13
Wittrock, M. C., **4:**12
Work portfolios, **3:**31
Work-sample assessment,
  3:26, **3:**81
Written expression, improving
  checklists, **9:**33–34
  defining, **10:**45
  familiar words, **9:**34–35
  focus on quantity, **9:**33
  self-evaluation, **9:**34
  software, **9:**35
  timed exercises, **9:**35
Wyatt v. Stickney, **2:**38 (tab)

Yell, M. L., **2:**19 (fig), **2:**29, **2:**49–50
Yost, D. S., **4:**5
Young, C .L., **9:**17
Youth apprenticeships programs,
    5:45, **5:**56
Ypsilanti Perry Preschool
    Project, **5:**15–16

Ysseldyke, J. E., **3:**14,
    3:23, **3:**71, **4:**5, **5:**18,
    6:9, **6:**33, **12:**62

Zobrest v. Catalina
    Foothills School
    District, **2:**43 (tab)

**CORWIN
PRESS**

The Corwin Press logo—a raven striding across an open book—represents the union of courage and learning. Corwin Press is committed to improving education for all learners by publishing books and other professional development resources for those serving the field of PreK–12 education. By providing practical, hands-on materials, Corwin Press continues to carry out the promise of its motto: **"Helping Educators Do Their Work Better."**